THE BRITISH LIBRARY
writers' lives

Mary Shelley

FRANKENSTEIN,

BY

MARY W. SHELLEY.

*The day of my departure at
length arrived.*

LONDON:

COLBURN AND BENTLEY,

NEW BURLINGTON STREET.

1831.

THE BRITISH LIBRARY
writers' lives

Mary Shelley

MARTIN GARRETT

OXFORD
UNIVERSITY PRESS

Contents

Mary Shelley

Maps showing places in England and Europe where Mary Shelley lived, travelled and wrote.

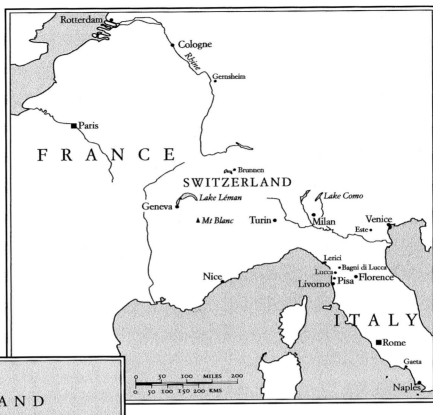

Mary Godwin: 'bold, somewhat imperious, and active of mind'

'It is not singular,' says Mary Shelley in her 1831 introduction to *Frankenstein*, 'that, as the daughter of two persons of distinguished literary celebrity, I should very early have thought of writing'. The 'distinguished' parents in question, William Godwin (1756–1836) and Mary Wollstonecraft (1759–97), not only wrote books but believed that they could, gradually at least, change the world by doing so.

Godwin and Wollstonecraft lived in a society where power, wealth and tradition still largely controlled nominally democratic politics and nominally equitable justice. In the book that made him famous – or, in conservative circles, notorious – *An Enquiry Concerning Political Justice* (1793), Godwin argues for the removal of such inequalities. This was to be achieved through reason, education, and individual improvement. A series of novels beginning with *Caleb Williams* (1794) make the same points in a form and style adapted to a wider readership, and were a stronger influence on his daughter, who also became a novelist of ideas.

Mary Wollstonecraft, like Godwin, hoped to reform society by the power of reasoned argument. In *A Vindication of the Rights of Woman* (1792) she makes the case that male 'superiority' is purely physical and that any apparent inferiority is mainly the result of a 'false system of education' which considers 'females rather as women than as human creatures' and encourages ignorance and superficiality. Wollstonecraft's experience of men tended to confirm her faith in women. She had defended her compliant mother against her bullying and improvident father, and her lover, the American businessman Gilbert Imlay, abandoned her and their infant daughter, Fanny, for another woman.

Wollstonecraft and Godwin first met briefly, and disliked each other, in 1791. But when they met again in 1796 they rapidly, and to the considerable surprise of people who knew them, became close friends and then lovers. Both were highly critical of the institution of marriage, but when she became pregnant she persuaded him that, in the present state of society, it was necessary to marry. Their daughter, Mary Wollstonecraft Godwin, was born at Somers Town, near London, on

30th August 1797. Only twelve days later Wollstonecraft died of puerperal fever – a common occurrence at a time when the medical profession was unaware that infection was introduced by the hands of doctors and midwives. Soon after her death Godwin combated his grief by writing a moving and honest account of her life, *Memoirs of the Author of 'The Rights of Woman'* (1798). He included accounts of Wollstonecraft's liaisons with Imlay and himself and her suicide attempts prompted by Imlay's disloyalty. The unintended consequence of such honesty was a scandal which took many years to die away. Many commentators decided that she was simply a 'prostitute', and that her views on female emancipation confirmed this. Godwin's own reputation had already suffered as part of a more general change in the English political climate. There had been a movement away from widespread sympathy with the ideals of the early phases of the French Revolution. The reformist views of writers like Godwin and Wollstonecraft met with increasing distrust or neglect once the Revolution had descended into bloodshed and England had embarked on twenty years of almost non-stop war with France.

Wollstonecraft's death left Godwin to look after his stepdaughter, Fanny, and his new daughter, Mary. Female friends and servants took over the practical side of caring for them, but Mary in particular developed for her father, from early childhood on, what she later described as 'an excessive and romantic attachment'. A less welcome influence came into Mary Godwin's life in 1801 when her father met and married their next-door neighbour, Mary Jane Clairmont. She already had two children; she described herself as a widow but in fact had not been married to either of the men who fathered her son Charles, born in 1795, and her daughter Jane, born in 1798. The marriage to Godwin took place because Clairmont, like Wollstonecraft before her, found herself pregnant. The child, named William, died at or soon after birth in April 1802. A second William was born in March 1803.

The marriage was, on the whole, a happy one for the couple involved. But the second Mrs Godwin had a habit of telling untruths which sometimes exasperated her husband and contributed to the distaste which many of his friends felt for her. Succeeding the venerated Wollstonecraft was not, of course, easy; her portrait by John Opie, on show in the study where Godwin received his visitors, perpetually invited comparisons. But the greatest tension appears to have been with her stepdaughter, Mary Godwin. Fanny was more docile, more easily dominated by the often forceful Mrs Godwin, and her own children did not suffer Mary's sense of displacement. From infancy Mary was evidently intelligent, spirited, and keenly aware of her own mother's superior intellectual status. Above all, stepmother and step-siblings came between Mary and her adored father. Conversely Mary Jane was still, many years later, accusing him of loving the adult Mary more than he loved her.

Mary Godwin later exaggerated how difficult life with her stepmother had been. It is clearly not true, as she gave the impression, that other members of the family were carefully educated while she and Fanny were left to do domestic chores. We know that all the girls learned French, Italian, and drawing, among other subjects, from the Godwins and a governess. Wollstonecraft might have laid more stress on the equality of the sexes, but the children were not kept in ignorance of such ideas; by their teens Mary and Jane were well versed in her work, and in 1812 or 1813 vigorously took the feminist side in a family discussion on whether 'women's vocation' should be 'purely domestic, or whether they should engage in outside interests'.

Godwin in particular encouraged the children to read and enquire widely, to learn where possible for themselves, and to use their imaginations. They were helped in these aims by some of his own books for children. Many of these were written for the Juvenile Library series, published by the bookselling business set up by the Godwins in 1805 to enable the family, with Godwin's books now unfashionable or politically suspect, to stay afloat financially. (When writing for children he used such pseudonyms as Edward Baldwin and Theophilus Marcliffe.) Instead of overloading

Mary Wollstonecraft Shelley as a child, engraved by Robert Hartley Cromek, 1850.

Private collection/Bridgeman Art Library

young minds with such inessential facts as 'from what part of the globe you receive every article of your furniture', he says in the introduction to his *Bible Stories* (1802), books for children should attend to 'those things which open the heart, which insensibly initiate the learner in the relations and generous offices of society, and enable him to put himself in imagination into the place of his neighbour, to feel his feelings, and to wish his wishes'.

Among the children's books published by the Godwins were *Tales from Shakespeare*, written by Mary Lamb with some assistance from her brother Charles, and Charles's *Adventures of Ulysses*. The Lambs were frequent visitors to Somers Town and then to 41 Skinner Street, where both the bookshop (on the ground floor) and the Godwins (on the upper floors) moved in 1807. Contact with them and Godwin's many other notable friends was probably at least as educative as reading the books. The composer Muzio Clementi, the painters James Northcote and Thomas Lawrence, the young radical essayist William Hazlitt, the scientist and poet Humphry Davy, and the surgeon and chemist Anthony Carlisle were among those who visited most often.

One visitor who made a particularly deep impression on the family was Samuel Taylor Coleridge, poet, philosopher and brilliant talker. If Godwin had an intellectual belief in the joys and the usefulness of imagination, Coleridge had a visionary sense of its transforming power. Godwin, not easily impressed as a rule, felt, when he first knew him, that in his charismatic company he was 'a purer, a more unreserved and natural being' than with anyone else. One evening – it may have been as early as 1804, since Coleridge was abroad between then and 1806 – he recited his poem 'The Ancient Mariner'. Jane and Mary (both aged only six or seven if the date was 1804) hid under the sofa and were discovered but allowed, at the poet's entreaty, to stay and listen. Long after Coleridge had, as far as Godwin and others were concerned, dissipated his youthful promise, the icy, eerie world of 'The Ancient Mariner' and its themes of responsibility and love stayed with Mary Shelley as an influence on *Frankenstein*.

Samuel Taylor Coleridge, aged thirty-two, in an engraving from James Northcote's portrait of 1804.

The British Library, London, pp54592

It is not surprising that, in such a setting, Mary wrote: 'As a child I scribbled; and my favourite pastime during the hours given me for recreation was to "write stories".' When she was fourteen and newly inspired by attending four of Coleridge's popular lectures on Shakespeare and Milton, she wrote weekly lectures of her own for her little brother to deliver; Aaron Burr, the disgraced former Vice-President of the United States, who had been drawn to Godwin's house in Skinner Street by his books and drawn back by the family's hospitality, heard William on 'The Influence of Government on the Character of the People'. After tea, Burr records, 'the girls' – Mary, Jane and possibly Fanny – 'sung and danced an hour'. No doubt they were keen to show their guest that their talents were not solely intellectual; a month earlier he had presented the three girls with silk stockings when they were about to go to a ball and had judged them, in their ballgowns, 'extremely neat, and with taste'.

Nevertheless Claire Clairmont (as Jane later called herself) could maintain with only some exaggeration – but much envy of her stepsister's achievements – that 'in our family if you cannot write an epic poem or a novel that by its originality knocks all other novels on the head, you are a despicable creature not worth acknowledging'.

Godwin was aware of the considerable potential of the daughter he described to an unknown correspondent as 'singularly bold, somewhat imperious, and active of mind', greatly desirous of knowledge, and almost invincibly persevering. But he seems often to have been somewhat distant as a father, at times ponderous and theoretical rather than spontaneously affectionate. One rather harsh comment survives: 'Tell Mary,' he says in a letter of May 1811 to his wife, 'that, in spite of unfavourable appearances, I have still faith that she will become a good and wise woman'. The thirteen-year-old girl had just gone with her stepmother to Ramsgate, on the Kent coast, because her hand had erupted with eczema or a similar condition and sea-bathing had been prescribed as part of her cure; it seems probable that the eruption was psychosomatic in origin.

Mary Godwin remained in Ramsgate for several months as a boarder at Miss Pettman's School. When she came back in December Burr noted that 'Mary has come home, and looks very lovely, but has not the air of strong health'. By March 1812, for whatever reason, her skin condition had flared up again, and this time the infection spread along one of her arms. Her doctor examined her again and recommended more salt-water bathing. This cannot, however, have been the only reason for Godwin's decision to send her on a long visit to stay with the family of his acquaintance William Baxter on the eastern Scottish coast. Presumably he thought that an extended time away from Skinner Street would help to dissipate family tension.

Mary Godwin sailed to Dundee. The journey took a week, during which the inexperienced traveller was sick, knew no one, and somehow was robbed of the money concealed in her corset. Life with the Baxters, however, turned out to be a fulfilling experience. Although they belonged to the Glassite church – a strict Protestant sect – family relationships were, especially when compared with those at Skinner Street, stable and relaxed. Isabella Baxter, four years older than Mary and a keen reader of Wollstonecraft, rapidly became her closest friend. A new landscape

A nineteenth-century scene of Dundee High Street. Mary Shelley paid two long visits to the Baxter family at nearby Broughty Ferry in 1812–14.

The British Library, London, 10369aaa40

opened up to what she later called her 'waking dreams'. The Baxters lived at Broughty Ferry, then several miles outside the city of Dundee, on the immensely broad estuary of the Tay. She saw her first mountains, the woods and waterfall near Dunkeld (later described in her novel *The Last Man*), and the ruined castle and cathedral at St Andrews. In Dundee and sailing past Broughty Ferry she saw whaling ships setting off on long and hazardous northern voyages – a reminder of 'The Ancient Mariner' and a possible influence on Robert Walton's expedition in *Frankenstein*. Altogether, as she later recalled in the 1831 introduction to *Frankenstein*, the 'northern shores of the Tay' might seem 'blank and dreary' but 'they were not so to me then. They were the eyrie of freedom, and the pleasant region where unheeded I could commune with the creatures of my fancy'. What she actually wrote at the time was 'in a most commonplace style,' she says, but

> It was beneath the trees of the grounds belonging to our house, or on the bleak sides of the woodless mountains near, that my true compositions, the airy flights of my imagination, were born and fostered. I did not make myself the heroine of my tales. Life appeared to me too commonplace an affair as regarded myself. I could not figure to myself that romantic woes or wonderful events would ever be my lot; but I was not confined to my own identity, and I could people the hours with creations far more interesting to me at that age than my own sensations.

≋ 'The irresistible wildness and sublimity of her feelings', 1814

Mary Godwin's participation in the world of woes and events began soon after her first return from Scotland in November 1812. (She went back to the Baxters' for a further nine months in June 1813.) The day after her arrival in London she dined, in Skinner Street, with guests including Percy Bysshe Shelley, a young and passionately idealistic admirer of Godwin's *Political Justice*. While Godwin had always believed in gradual reform of society, his disciple wanted more immediate action. He quarrelled with his respectable country land-owning father. He wrote *The Necessity of Atheism* with his friend Thomas Jefferson Hogg and was consequently expelled from Oxford university in 1811. Then, in February 1812, he rushed off to Ireland to preach and disseminate pamphlets against poverty, injustice, and restrictions on free assembly. Shelley's failure to win much support, his habitual restlessness, and Godwin's forceful letters warning against the violence he was in danger of stirring up, combined to bring him back from Ireland in April. Thereafter he directed his radicalism more often into poetry than into activism. His long poem *Queen Mab*, energetically attacking monarchy, war, commerce and religion, was printed privately in 1813.

William Godwin was genuinely interested in Shelley's ideas and happy to act as a mentor. But the fact that Godwin was by now in dire financial straits also influenced his interest; the bookshop and publishing venture were not flourishing, and he kept out of debtors' prison only with the aid of last-minute loans and benefactions. Godwin believed firmly that it was the duty of anyone with surplus money to give it to those – himself in this case – called upon to advance justice and enlightenment. Shelley freely agreed with this view. And although he was not himself rich, his future prospects were good enough for money-lenders to take a risk with large sums of money. During the spring and summer of 1814 a package was negotiated whereby Shelley obtained £2,240 by signing a bond to repay some £8,000 when he came into his inheritance at the death of his father. Godwin believed that the whole of the sum raised was destined for him.

Opposite page:

Percy Bysshe Shelley *by the Shelleys' friend Amelia Curran. According to his friend Thomas Jefferson Hogg 'he always looked, wild, intellectual, unearthly; like a spirit that has just descended from the sky; like a demon risen that moment out of the ground'.*

National Portrait Gallery, London

Shelley was always searching for like-minded people, or people whom he might render like-minded. Usually they were female. In 1811, with characteristic impetuosity, he had eloped with Harriet Westbrook, a sixteen-year-old schoolfriend of his sisters. In 1813 the relationship between husband and wife began to break down and they had spent several periods living apart by the time Shelley met Mary Godwin for the second time on 5th May 1814. He was twenty-one and she was sixteen.

St Pancras churchyard, in an engraving of 1816. As a child Mary Godwin frequently visited her mother's grave here.

The British Library, London, 294.i.10

It did not seem unnatural to the Godwins that their daughters went for walks with the interesting young idealist. They walked often to an arbour in Charterhouse Square and to Mary Wollstonecraft's grave in St Pancras churchyard – simply reaffirming their reformist ideals there, the Godwins probably assumed. As Shelley and Mary Godwin became more intimate (while Jane Clairmont paced up and down at a discreet distance), he told Mary of his incompatibility with Harriet and claimed that she had been unfaithful to him. He may or may not actually have believed this.

In his own view, besides, he was acting quite justifiably since, as he put it in the notes to *Queen Mab*, 'Love withers under constraint; its very essence is liberty'. Mary Godwin was happy to listen; her father, after all, had once believed that marriage was 'the most odious of all monopolies'. They declared their love for each other on 26th June; Shelley had vacillated, tried until then to conceal his 'ardent passion', he wrote to Hogg, but she, inspired by the spirit of truth, had, in the 'sublime and rapturous moment when she declared herself mine', dispelled his doubts. Probably either that day or the following they had sex for the first time. Tradition affirms that this took place in St Pancras churchyard.

As the visits to Wollstonecraft's tomb attest, Mary Godwin appealed to Shelley on the grounds of her heritage as well as herself. She seemed almost to embody the excitement of her parents' ideas, but without losing her own strong identity: 'the originality and loveliness of Mary's character', he told Hogg, 'was apparent to me from her very motions and tones of voice. The irresistible wildness and sublimity of her feelings showed itself in her gestures and her looks – Her smile, how persuasive it was and how pathetic! She is gentle, to be convinced and tender; yet not incapable of ardent imagination and hatred'. (Hatred of injustice and those perceived as unjust was a virtue as Shelley saw it; she very probably expressed her antipathy for her stepmother in these terms as well as attacking such less personal foes as conventional religion or the treatment of the poor.) Her appeal was also, of course, more simply physical. Although there is no certainly identified picture of her at this time, we do have Claire Clairmont's later word-picture of Mary Godwin's hair: 'Mary's hair is light brown, of a sunny and burnished brightness like the autumnal foliage when played upon by the rays of the setting sun; it sets in round her face and falls upon her shoulders in gauzy wavings and is so fine it looks as if the wind had tangled it together into golden network'.

One other recollection neatly combines the two sorts of appeal: the hero-worship and the physical attraction. Thomas Jefferson Hogg recalled his first glimpse of Mary at Skinner Street, many years after the event, in a passage of his 1858 life of Shelley: 'A very young female, fair and fair-haired, pale indeed, and with a piercing look, wearing a frock of tartan'. Hogg asked if she was Godwin's daughter and Shelley told him that she was 'The daughter of Godwin and Mary'.

Mary Shelley

What so appealed to Mary Godwin about Shelley must on the whole be surmised, since she kept no journal at the time and none of her letters from this period survives. But she too was clearly attracted by a man who seemed as intellectually strong and fearless and untrammelled – if Harriet and the child could somehow be excluded from the equation – as her father had been in the 1790s. She was drawn to him by his eloquence, his enthusiasms, and the 'wild, intellectual, unearthly' looks described by Hogg. He also offered the possibility of escape from Skinner Street: an escape from a stepmother who must have seemed all the more irritating after the Scottish adventure, perhaps even from a father beloved but much harassed by money matters and, subconsciously at least, a little disappointing.

Events moved swiftly. On 6th July Shelley, to Godwin's complete amazement and horror, announced that he was in love with his daughter and intended to take her abroad. Godwin had suspected nothing because, as he wrote to Shelley nearly a fortnight later,

> I trusted to your principles ... nor did I fear more for the principles of my child. ... I could not fear that the existence of your wife and child could be overlooked by either of you. ... I could not believe that you would sacrifice your own character and usefulness, the happiness of an innocent and meritorious wife, and the fair and spotless fame of my young child to fierce impulse of passion. – I could not believe that you would enter my house under the name of benefactor, to leave behind an endless poison to corrode my soul.

As far as he was concerned this was a very different situation from the one in which he and Wollstonecraft, unmarried and mature, had entered on their pre-marital liaison. Besides, having experienced the vilification of Wollstonecraft once her extra-marital involvements had become common knowledge, Godwin was particularly anxious to preserve his daughter's 'fame' or reputation. If her relations with Shelley were known or even suspected, not only her future place in society but that of all her family and especially Jane and Fanny would be endangered. He also feared, as more modern fathers might, that only misery could result from a girl of sixteen running off with a man she barely knew.

Godwin summoned up all his powers of persuasion against what to him was this 'licentious love'. For a while he seemed to have succeeded. He saw Harriet and told her he would try to save her marriage. The Godwins managed to keep the lovers apart for a week or so. But contact was maintained, since Jane Clairmont and then the bookshop porter smuggled into Skinner Street letters from Shelley and a copy of *Queen Mab*. And then, according to the admittedly unreliable Mrs Godwin, he rushed into the house brandishing a pistol and a bottle of laudanum and encouraged his beloved to kill herself with him so that they could at least be united in death. He was successfully ejected but, Mrs Godwin claimed, nearly succeeded in killing himself with an overdose of laudanum a week later.

On 28th July Godwin made a laconic journal entry: 'Five in the Morning'. At that time Mary Godwin and Jane Clairmont – her accomplice throughout the preceding weeks – had slipped out of the house, dressed discreetly in black silk gowns and bonnets, to join Shelley in a hired coach. Clairmont would be useful on their European travels since she prided herself on speaking French better than the others. She also shared their scorn for convention, and no doubt felt that restrictions would be imposed on her freedom if she stayed behind. And she was clearly herself attracted to, or very interested in, Shelley. They travelled to Dover and crossed, in a small boat and heavy seas, to Calais. Mrs Godwin pursued them to Dessein's Hotel. The following morning she went home, defeated. Shelley, doubtless to Mary's unkind glee, turned her into a stereotypically comic figure in the lovers' joint journal: a Captain Davison 'came and told us that a fat lady had arrived, who said that I had run away with her daughter'.

Now the adventure could begin. It had been made possible by a greater defeat than that of the Godwins: Napoleon Bonaparte's abdication as emperor in April brought peace between Britain and its allies and France for the first time since 1803. Visitors were flocking towards Paris in the hope of taking up their old fashionable amusements under the restored monarchy of Louis XVIII. Shelley and his companions had different preoccupations. They took with them a portable library including several of the works of Wollstonecraft. And their main destination was not Paris but Uri in Switzerland, because Jane Clairmont believed this to be the home of her maternal ancestors and because it was a setting in Godwin's novel *Fleetwood*. As usual, they lived not a little through their books.

The reality of foreign travel without funds was, inevitably, different from the ideal. The group could not proceed beyond Paris until Shelley had managed, with some difficulty, to negotiate a loan of £60 from a certain Tavernier. They bought a donkey to carry the luggage; Shelley noted, ruefully, that 'We set out to Charenton in the evening carrying the ass who was weak and unfit for labour'. They replaced it with a mule. This was strong enough to bear the bags and one rider, but Shelley sprained his leg and was obliged to ride all day. After only four days they sold the

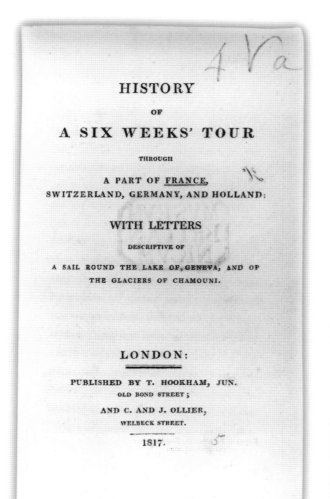

HISTORY

OF

A SIX WEEKS' TOUR

THROUGH

A PART OF FRANCE,

SWITZERLAND, GERMANY, AND HOLLAND:

WITH LETTERS

DESCRIPTIVE OF

A SAIL ROUND THE LAKE OF GENEVA, AND OF
THE GLACIERS OF CHAMOUNI.

LONDON:

PUBLISHED BY T. HOOKHAM, JUN.
OLD BOND STREET;

AND C. AND J. OLLIER,
WELBECK STREET.

1817.

IT is now nearly three years since this Journey took place, and the journal I then kept was not very copious; but I have so often talked over the incidents that befel us, and attempted to describe the scenery through which we passed, that I think few occurrences of any interest will be omitted.

We left London July 28th, 1814, on a hotter day than has been known in this climate for many years. I am not

B

mule and hired a 'voiture' or open carriage. These transactions swiftly ate into the £60. Soon they entered areas of France where people's sufferings were much worse than sprains or insolvency: villages sacked by the Cossacks in the closing battles of the war only a few months previously. In *History of a Six Weeks' Tour* (1817) Mary Godwin says that 'The distress of the inhabitants, whose houses had been burned, their cattle killed, and all their wealth destroyed, has given a sting to my detestation of war, which none can feel who have not travelled through a country pillaged and wasted by this plague, which, in his pride, man inflicts upon his fellow'. But at the time, to judge from her journal entries, she was less disposed to sympathise with the

The opening of the Shelleys' anonymously published History of a Six Weeks' Tour.

The British Library, London, C.58.b.12

inhabitants. With the easy rapidity of judgement of the first-time visitor she declared the French dirty and inhospitable.

Switzerland was beautiful and Shelley obtained more cash from a banker in Neuchâtel, but the house they found at Brunnen (in Uri) was cold, ugly and expensive and after a couple of days, with only £28 remaining, the three travellers decided to set off for home. They journeyed, by Rhine boat, carriage and coach, through Germany to Rotterdam. There was no money left but they persuaded the captain of a vessel sailing to Gravesend to accept payment after their passage. On 13th September they proceeded by boat to London where, eventually, Shelley persuaded the long-suffering Harriet to hand over the necessary £20. She had so far been unimpressed by his suggestions that she should simply join the group.

Altogether it is easy to make this first foreign expedition sound fairly disastrous. But the relationship between the lovers was strengthened by their mixed experiences abroad. They kept the journal together and began the programme of intensive reading, often aloud, which would continue for much of their time together. Shelley dictated part of his unfinished eastern romance 'The Assassins' to Mary Godwin and they probably discussed together the story, 'Hate' (now lost), which she wrote in Holland at the end of the trip. Conceivably they also had an experience of longer term literary significance: when their boat moored overnight at Gernsheim on the Rhine on 2nd September the lovers walked (without Jane) for three hours. If they walked in the right direction they might have come within sight of Castle Frankenstein; possibly they also heard and remembered local legends connected with Konrad Dippel, an eighteenth-century physician, born in the castle, who was famous for his attempts to reanimate corpses.

London and 'enshadowing thickets', 1814–16

The inconveniences of travel were soon forgotten amid the complications of life back in London. The Godwins, to Mary's surprise and distress, refused the lovers entry to the family home and were prepared to take Jane Clairmont back only if she repudiated her fellow runaways. Godwin even ignored them in the street. (His daughter liked to believe that this was a result mainly of his wife's pernicious influence: 'she plagues [him] out of his life', she assured Shelley.) Shelley plunged steadily deeper into debt. He was still unreconciled with his father. He was financially involved with Harriet and their fifteen-month-old daughter, Ianthe (soon followed by a son, Charles, born in November 1814), and needed to provide for the now clearly pregnant Mary and for Jane. And he was determined in spite of it all to raise money for Godwin. Often Shelley was on the move, avoiding his creditors' agents. Between 23rd October and 8th November 1814 he lived mostly apart from Mary Godwin, able only to meet her briefly and furtively except between midnight on Saturdays and midnight on Sundays, the only period when, legally, he could not be arrested for debt. The couple's surviving letters of this period are full both of practical arrangements and desperate assurances of love. Twenty years later, in her novel *Lodore*, Mary recreated their situation fairly closely for her characters Edward and Ethel Villiers.

One aspect of Shelley and Mary Godwin's experience was not, however, shared by the Villiers couple; there is no equivalent in *Lodore* to Jane Clairmont. Clairmont, who now decided to be known by her actual first name Clara and then as Claire, had literary aspirations, although she lacked her stepsister's ability and prestigious parentage. She was also involved in a close, if probably not sexually intimate, relationship with Shelley. Inevitably there was a degree of jealousy between the two young women. They were forced to live in irritating proximity at the various London lodgings between which the group moved, and even the lovers' nights – when Shelley was there – were sometimes interrupted by Clairmont's attacks of 'horrors'. Shelley could not resist experimenting with how easily he could bring on these fits by telling her frightening tales. His intense interest in her, and power over her, prolonged the difficulties of the tripartite relationship by making her too dependent on him. He had always – even as a child, with his sisters – liked to lead or engage with a predominantly female group, and one of his, Claire Clairmont's and Mary Godwin's favourite books at this time was *The Empire of the Nairs*, in which James Lawrence imagined an Indian community where women had equal rights with men, sex was free and uninhibited, and nudity a matter of course.

To enjoy reading such works was, especially in the early nineteenth century, usually a long step from putting their theories into practice. Mary Godwin, for instance, had been outraged when Shelley proposed that she should bathe naked in a French stream. And if she was willing, reluctantly, to consider cooperating when Hogg, with Shelley's knowledge and approval, proposed that their friendship should become sexual in early 1815, she clearly decided against it in the end. Initially she was able to use delaying tactics – she held out some hope to Hogg but said he must wait until after the birth of her child. The baby, a daughter, was born prematurely in February 1814 but died less than two weeks later. Mary wrote at once to ask 'My dearest Hogg' to come because 'you are so calm a creature'. He stayed with the family during the whole of his lawyer's vacation that spring, but his role seems to have remained that of soother rather than lover. (Radical theory could not, besides, change the fact that she evidently did not find Hogg physically attractive.)

A temporary solution to the problem of Claire Clairmont, or 'the lady', as Mary Godwin caustically described her, was found in May 1815. After a period of even greater tension than usual, Clairmont went to live at Lynmouth in Devon. There was a last conversation between 'Shelley and his friend', Mary noted in her journal, which Shelley, who still sometimes wrote in it, was likely to read. But on 13th May, in more positive mood, she celebrated Claire's absence and the hope of more uninterrupted closeness with Shelley by leaving blank the last eight pages in order to 'begin a new journal with our regeneration'. Financially, too, there was reason now for some optimism. On the same day as Claire's departure Shelley's father agreed to a settlement paying his debts and granting him an income of £1,000 a year. Godwin would receive £1,000 of the sum Shelley had promised him and Harriet would receive £200 at once and annually thereafter. (Godwin remained angry, however, that he did not receive the full £2,240 he had expected.)

In early August 1815 Shelley and Mary Godwin, now pregnant again, moved into a furnished house at Bishopsgate, the eastern entrance to Windsor Great Park. In this area – in Windsor Castle and its 'enshadowing thickets' – the main characters in her novel of 1826, *The Last Man*, spend their happiest days. Shelley was more immediately inspired by the Great Park, whose 'magnificent woodland', Mary recalled, 'was a fitting study to inspire the various descriptions of forest-scenery' in his poem *Alastor; or the Spirit of Solitude*. She herself wrote nothing that we know of during the Bishopsgate period. This year she was, as usual, engaged in an intensive programme of reading: works ranging from Ovid's *Metamorphoses* to Rousseau's *Confessions* and novels by her father. She often re-read books by her parents, partly to confirm her sense that she was living in accordance with their beliefs – or in Godwin's case his original beliefs. It was also a way of maintaining a sense of contact

Virginia Water, a landscaped lake to the South of Windsor Great Park, engraved by Robert Wallis for Mary Shelley's story 'The Mourner' in The Keepsake for 1830. *She lived nearby, at Bishopsgate, in 1815–16.*

The British Library, London, pp6670

with her lost mother and estranged father. This sense might be extended if she could write something worthy of them and of her lover, of whose poetic genius she from the beginning had no doubt and who, she says in the *Frankenstein* introduction, was 'very anxious that I should prove myself worthy of my parentage, and enrol myself on the page of fame'.

Claire Clairmont too was keen to make her mark. In consequence, she wrote to Lord Byron, the most famous and fashionable poet of the day, in March or early April 1816. She worked, in a series of letters, to whet his interest. She asked for advice on a possible acting career, described and then sent her manuscript novel, and carefully indicated her Shelley and Godwin links. Finally he agreed to meet her. She offered him sex and, having tried to warn her off, he accepted because, as he later told a friend, 'if a girl of eighteen comes prancing to you at all hours – there is but one way'. He had already decided to leave England following the rapid and scandalous breakdown of his ill-advised marriage to Annabella Milbanke; when he sailed for the continent a few days later he left Clairmont keen to pursue him, triumphant at her success and, she was yet to learn, pregnant.

For once the famous connection was Claire's, not Mary Godwin's. She was able proudly to introduce Byron to her, probably on 21st April, the day after the liaison began, without at this stage explaining that the relationship was sexual. Mary was, it seems, favourably impressed by the man so many people wanted to meet. 'She perpetually exclaims "How mild he is! how gentle! So different from what I expected…",' Clairmont reported. Probably Mary Godwin had expected to encounter a moody and melancholy 'Byronic hero' – a part the author did sometimes like to play. Mary's lifelong fascination with Byron had begun.

Claire Clairmont had been living in London again since January. Mary Godwin and Shelley settled there in March with their baby, William, born on 24th January and named after his grandfather William Godwin in the hope of

reconciliation. Partly at Clairmont's prompting the group decided to go abroad again. They could re-live the 1814 expedition and, with the aid of more funds, improve on it. Clairmont could follow Byron to Geneva and perhaps become established as his long-term mistress; either she did not know much about his restless promiscuity or she felt that she was the woman who could captivate him out of it. The others, who like her were attentive readers of Byron's poems and interested to

This painting shows Geneva, on the shores of Lake Léman, as painted by Jean Dubois. Mary Godwin, Shelley and Clairmont returned there in 1816.

Fine Art Society/Bridgeman Art Gallery

29

George Gordon, Lord Byron, in 1814, aged twenty-six. Portrait by Thomas Phillips.

Nottingham City Museums and Art Galleries (Newstead Abbey)

know more of him and his philosophy of life, were content to accompany her. Godwin, coming home from a trip to Edinburgh, was displeased and worried at Shelley's latest sudden departure; Shelley tried to placate him with an unfulfillable promise of £300 over the summer. But the group was relieved to leave behind the pressure of Godwin's disapproval and seek, like Byron, a less morally censorious environment in Switzerland.

Switzerland and 'the component parts of a creature', 1816

In fact scandal was, at times, difficult to avoid. Tourists in Geneva enjoyed training telescopes on Byron's villa in the hope of seeing something shocking. Shelley's party was much less well known, but there was some likelihood of notoriety for a man travelling with two young women and with a defiant habit of proclaiming himself, in hotel registers, 'Democrat, Philanthropist and Atheist'. (All three words had dangerous radical connotations. Shelley wrote them in Greek, but Byron still felt it prudent to try to erase them from one of the registers he came upon.) And once the Shelley group joined Byron there was all the greater opportunity for gossip and innuendo. One British visitor, Lord Glenbervie, noted in his diary, somewhat confusedly, that Byron was cohabiting with 'a Mrs Shelley, wife to the man who keeps the Mount Coffee House'. (In reality it was Harriet Shelley's father who was the retired proprietor of the coffee-house in question.) Others believed firmly that Byron was living with two women; their telescopes, as Byron said, 'must have had very distorted optics'.

The two women, Shelley and the baby arrived at Hôtel d'Angleterre, Sécheron, near Geneva, in mid-May. About ten days later Byron also reached the hotel. Claire Clairmont was frustrated that he did not immediately rush to make contact, but she succeeded in renewing sexual relations at least occasionally during the rest of the summer. Often, however, Shelley and friends, Byron, and his young doctor and companion John William Polidori, interacted as a larger group. On 27th May Byron had waded ashore from his boat to be introduced to Shelley. Soon afterwards the two groups moved across the lake. First the Shelleys (Mary Godwin was known here, as Lord Glenbervie's tale attests, as Mrs Shelley) and Clairmont rented Maison Chapuis at Montalègre, near Cologny, a lakeside cottage with a view of the 'dark frowning Jura' mountains, 'behind whose range we every evening see the sun sink'. Byron and Polidori then came to the somewhat grander Villa Diodati, with its terraced garden, balcony with wide views of the lake, Geneva, and the Jura, and associations with an earlier English poet, John Milton, whose republican politics as

Villa Diodati, which Byron rented in the summer of 1816. The conversations that inspired elements of Frankenstein *took place here.*

John Murray

well as his work were important to the travellers. The villa could be reached easily from the cottage by walking up through a sloping vineyard.

It was at Villa Diodati that some of the most famous conversations in literary history took place. Late one rainy night, probably 15th June, the five adults 'crowded around a blazing wood fire', according to the preface Shelley wrote for *Frankenstein* in 1818, and read ghost stories from *Fantasmagoriana*, a German collection translated into French. 'These tales excited in us a playful desire of imitation.' The 'illustrious poets', says Mary Shelley in her introduction of 1831, started stories but, 'annoyed by the platitude of prose, speedily relinquished their uncongenial task'. Polidori also embarked on a tale as, possibly, did Clairmont. Only Mary Godwin could not, at first, find the inspiration for a story, 'one which would speak to the mysterious fears of our nature and awaken thrilling horror – one to make the reader dread to look round, to curdle the blood, and quicken the beatings of the heart'.

Every morning she had to confess that she still could not think of a story. But soon after the launching of the ghost story competition, or possibly some time before it, there was another conversation at Villa Diodati with Mary Godwin (and, no doubt, Claire Clairmont, 'a devout but nearly silent listener'). Byron and Shelley talked about 'the nature and the principle of life, and whether there was any probability of its ever being discovered and communicated'. Among other possibilities, 'perhaps a corpse would be reanimated' with the aid of electricity, or 'perhaps the component parts of a creature might be manufactured, brought together, and endued with vital warmth'. According to Polidori's diary it was he and Shelley who were the speakers; it is quite possible that Mary Shelley, writing fifteen years later, misremembered or skilfully rearranged events and conversations at Diodati. (Tantalisingly, her journal for this period is lost.) However this may be, such discussions had an obvious effect on the story and concerns of *Frankenstein*. 'Night waned upon this talk', Mary Shelley continues:

> *When I placed my head on my pillow, I did not sleep, nor could I be said to think. My imagination, unbidden, possessed and guided me, gifting the successive images that arose in my mind with a vividness far beyond the usual bounds of reverie. I saw – with shut eyes, but acute mental vision – I saw the pale student of unhallowed arts kneeling beside the thing he had put together. I saw the hideous phantasm of a man stretched out, and then, on the working of some powerful engine, show signs of life, and stir with an uneasy, half-vital motion. ... His success would terrify the artist; he would rush away from his odious handiwork. ... He sleeps; but he is awakened; he opens his eyes; behold, the horrid thing stands at his bedside, opening his curtains and looking on him with yellow, watery, but speculative eyes.*

She opened her own eyes in terror, she says, wanting 'to exchange the ghastly images of my fancy for the realities' of the room, 'the dark *parquet*, the closed shutters, with the moonlight struggling through, and the sense I had that the glassy lake and white high Alps were beyond'. To escape from her hideous imagining she tried thinking instead about her 'tiresome, unlucky ghost story'. If only she could frighten the reader as much as she had just been frightened. And so, of course, it dawned on her that her waking dream was the very thing; 'I need only describe the spectre which had haunted my midnight pillow'. She could at last announce that she had '*thought of a story*'; one which, it turned out, would have the power of myth, of archetype, for her own and succeeding generations.

She began to develop the main plot of *Frankenstein* while the 'illustrious poets' spent a week taking the boat they shared (moored usually in the small harbour near Maison Chapuis) around the Lake. It is, as befits a tale so often subsequently taken up and reworked, a simple plot. Victor Frankenstein, a student of natural philosophy,

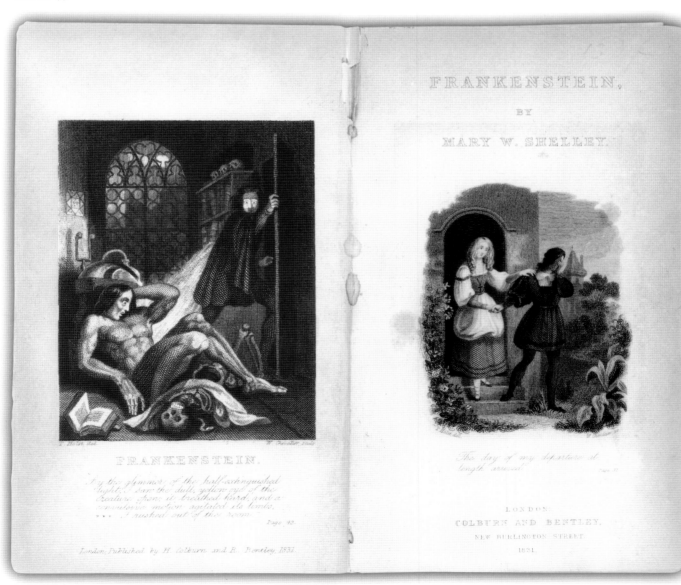

finds a way – not specified in detail – of animating the creature or monster he has put together from 'bones from charnel-houses' and materials from 'the dissecting-room and the slaughter-house'. Horrified by the result, he abandons the creature, who stumbles out of the house and away into the woods. Rejected for his hideousness by the people he encounters, the creature seeks revenge on the man who, by making and neglecting him, inflicted this suffering. He comes upon Frankenstein's young brother William and kills him. He confronts Frankenstein and demands that he create a mate for him, to end his loneliness. Frankenstein's failure to do this leads to new killings, including that of his bride, Elizabeth, on their wedding night. He pursues the monster but eventually dies before he can catch him. The monster, even more alone in the world without his creator, goes off 'to collect my funeral pile, and consume to ashes this miserable frame'.

Behind this story lay much more than the eager debates at Villa Diodati, although these helped to focus the eighteen-year-old author's already extraordinarily wide reading and thinking. Her awareness of recent discussions and developments in science, for instance, derives probably from her personal acquaintance with the controversial biologist William Lawrence (also Shelley's physician and a friend of Godwin) and certainly from reading such works as Sir Humphry Davy's *Discourse ... on Chemistry* (1802). Davy proclaims that chemistry grants man powers 'which may almost be called creative; which have enabled him to modify and change the beings surrounding him, and by his experiments to interrogate nature with power, not simply as a scholar ... but rather as a master, active with his own instruments'. She had evidently read or heard about the late-eighteenth and early-nineteenth-century experiments by Luigi Galvani, Giovanni Aldini and others in which an electric charge made corpses move an arm or a leg, giving the illusion or the promise of reanimation. She must have talked about such matters with Shelley, whose fascination with electricity went back to the lectures he heard, while still at school, from Adam Walker, one of the scientists who believed that life itself was sparked off by electricity.

At times *Frankenstein*, as the author's 'hideous imagining' and the novel's later reputation suggest, has more to do with traditions of horror than of science: the huge and ugly monster lit by lightning after the murder of William, or bounding across the ice 'with superhuman speed' before his confrontation with Frankenstein, or grinning and jeering through the window at Elizabeth's strangled corpse. Mary Godwin had read of wicked, crazed villains and innocent young heroines in Gothic novels including Ann Radcliffe's *The Mysteries of Udolpho* and Matthew Lewis's *The Monk*. 'Monk' Lewis himself stayed at Villa Diodati in mid-August, about two months into the composition of *Frankenstein*. She did not actually meet him, but Shelley was sufficiently taken with five supernatural stories, 'all grim', which Lewis told him, to write them into the joint journal.

At Diodati two months earlier, probably one or two days after she 'thought of a story', horror made a more direct appearance, according to Polidori's diary, when Byron recited from Coleridge's *Christabel*. He reached the lines concerning 'the witch's breast' – the revelation that Geraldine, seemingly a helpless 'damsel bright,/Drest in a silken robe of white' is in fact some kind of evil being. After a moment of silence 'Shelley, shrieking and putting his hands to his head, ran out of the room with a candle'. Once Dr Polidori had calmed the patient down he explained that he 'was looking at Mrs S, & suddenly thought of a woman he had heard of who had eyes instead of nipples, which, taking hold of his mind, horrified him'. The response of 'Mrs S' to his sudden horror is not known, but it probably contributed something to her thinking on how to 'frighten my reader as I myself had been frightened' and the deathly Geraldine's 'bosom and half her side/...lean and old and foul of hue' possibly had some influence on the yellow skin and 'shrivelled complexion' of the monster, than whom 'a mummy again endued with animation' could not be more hideous.

But the creation of horror is not Mary Shelley's main aim in *Frankenstein*. The examples of the monster's horrific conduct and appearance given above come, significantly, from Frankenstein's narrative of events. It is he who insists that his creation is a 'monster' (twenty-seven times), 'fiend' (twenty-five), 'daemon' (eighteen), 'wretch' (fifteen); he calls him, somewhat more neutrally, a 'creature', only sixteen times. Certainly the terrible consequences of Frankenstein neglecting his responsibility towards his creation are apparent from early in the novel. But the strength of the case Frankenstein must answer becomes clear only when the creature eventually has the chance to put his own point of view both to Frankenstein and to

A page from the rough draft of Frankenstein *in which the creature begins his narrative.*

Bodleian Library, Oxford, Dep.c.534/1

the reader. The reversal is extraordinary: not only can this mummy-like monster, this killer of young William, speak – as not in some later versions of the story – but he is articulate, intelligent, logical. He speaks, impassioned but dignified, of his misery and sense of abandonment:

Oh, Frankenstein, be not equitable to every other, and trample upon me alone, to whom thy justice, and even thy clemency and affection, is most due. Remember, that I am thy creature: I ought to be thy Adam; but I am rather the fallen angel, whom thou drivest from joy for no misdeed. Everywhere I see bliss, from which alone I am irrevocably excluded. I was benevolent and good; misery made me a fiend. Make me happy, and I shall again be virtuous.

He has, in circumstances he will soon explain, read Milton's *Paradise Lost* (1667), from which he draws both something of the resonant quality of his speech and the contrast between the original good relationship between God and Adam and the feelings of the 'fallen angel' Satan, excluded from the 'bliss' of Eden.

The creator Frankenstein goes to hear out his creature in a mountain hut. The creature's narrative, taking us back to the time immediately after his animation, begins. Having lived for a time in the woods, existing at first on berries, nuts, and roots, he gradually discovers the moon, birdsong, and fire. When he enters a village the frightened inhabitants shriek, run away, or throw stones at him, but in a 'hovel' or covered wooden enclosure attached to a cottage he finds 'a shelter, however miserable, from the inclemency of the season, and still more from the barbarity of man'.

From his refuge he watches the cottagers (De Lacey, an old, blind man, his son Felix and his daughter Agatha), and continues his education in human character and emotions. By listening to them he slowly begins to learn their language, a process which is accelerated when they are joined by a foreign young woman, Safie, who herself needs to be taught the language. He is also helped when Felix reads one book, Volney's *Ruins of Empire*, aloud, and when he rather conveniently finds in the woods three others which carry forward his understanding of human bonds and affections, cruelty and injustice, and potential for good or evil, inclusion or exclusion: *Paradise Lost*, Plutarch's *Lives*, and Goethe's *Sorrows of Young Werther*. Like much of the creature's narrative, this is all fairly implausible but it seems much less so in the reading because he speaks in such a convinced, rational tone; everything he says is aimed to persuade Frankenstein and the reader to appreciate his position. And he describes his growth into knowledge with marked intellectual curiosity, like a scientist with more laudable interests, more interest in human beings, than his maker.

The monster longs to share the De Laceys' family life, which makes him painfully aware of his own lack of such ties. He knows that Frankenstein, the one person who could have been expected to love and nurture him, has abandoned him. His admiration for the cottagers, clearly moral heroes compared with the irresponsible Frankenstein, grows as he learns their story. The De Laceys have been exiled from France, and their property confiscated, because Felix helped an unjustly condemned Turkish merchant to escape from prison in Paris and conducted him and his daughter, Safie, into Italy. Felix and Safie had fallen in love and the merchant had agreed that they would marry, but when he heard that Felix 'was deprived of his wealth and rank' he 'became a traitor to good feeling and honour' and ordered his daughter to prepare to return to her native country. She set off instead to find her beloved Felix and, after many difficulties, reached the cottage.

Mary Godwin almost certainly completed the first version of the Safie material at Bath in December 1816. We know that between 6th and 9th of this month she was re-reading her mother's *Vindication of the Rights of Woman*, and Safie (at first named Maimouna or Amina, but re-named so as to suggest 'Sophia' – Wisdom) is one of the characters who most obviously draws attention to the novel's feminist perspective. Safie's late mother taught her daughter 'to aspire to higher powers of intellect' and 'independence of spirit'. 'This lady', like Wollstonecraft, 'died; but her lessons were indelibly impressed on the mind of Safie'.

Safie escapes from a patriarchal society but women in *Frankenstein* more generally remain, whether or not they realise it, dominated by men. Frankenstein loves Elizabeth, but some of the terms in which he chooses to express his love are strikingly patronising or possessive. In childhood, while he 'admired her understanding' and imagination, he 'loved to tend on her, as I should on a favourite animal'. And in the 1831 revision when his mother says playfully 'I have a pretty present for my Victor' and introduces him to Elizabeth, 'I, with childish seriousness, interpreted her words literally, and looked upon Elizabeth as mine – mine to protect, love, and cherish. All praises bestowed on her, I received as made to a possession of my own'.

Later his attitude is presented as more unequivocally self-centred: he neglects Elizabeth while he obsessively pursues his ambition to create life, he fails to tell her about the monster and its effect on his behaviour, he fails to protect her on their wedding night, when it has not for a moment occurred to him that the monster's threat to be there on that occasion could menace her as much as him. Another woman, the family servant Justine Moritz, perishes at least partly through male pride. She is wrongly accused of the murder of William and condemned to hang. Frankenstein knows that she is innocent, but feels that a declaration to the court that he is the guilty party because he created the killer would be 'considered as the ravings of a madman'. This may sound a reasonable consideration, but the degree of Frankenstein's focus on himself rather than Justine is further underlined by his surprising statement that, when he rushed out of the courtroom in despair, 'The tortures of the accused did not equal mine'. Elizabeth, by contrast, speaks to the court eloquently, if unsuccessfully, in Justine's defence.

Many readers have speculated that the author saw herself, too, as a victim of male dominance, as Shelley's creature or her father's. More certainly, there are parallels between the position of the creature and of women, no doubt to some extent including the female author. Both are easily excluded; the ancient philosopher Aristotle had even said that to be female is to be, in a sense, 'deformed'. Most nineteenth-century men would not have agreed with him, but most women were still almost as effectively blocked from positions of leadership, esteem, and decision-making, as the monster in his hovel. Women were usually defined by their position as men's kinsfolk, wives, or mistresses, and the monster's only real hope of achieving any kind of status or relationship is through his creator, his master. The hopelessness of his situation is increased by Frankenstein's desertion of the traditionally feminine side of human nature. Significantly his loving mother dies just before he embarks on his secretive and misdirected studies at the university of Ingolstadt. During his time there he fails to communicate with Elizabeth, to whom the dying mother explicitly passed on her nurturing role in the Frankenstein family. In constructing his creature he replaces the natural process of conception and pregnancy, and his failure to nourish and care for his offspring is in line with this. (Mary Godwin's own baby was five months old when she started work on *Frankenstein*.)

Moved and encouraged by everything he knows about the virtuous De Laceys and independent Safie, the monster decides, after a year, to risk revealing himself to them. While the others are out he goes in and tells the blind father that he is a friendless stranger; there are people who might help him, but 'where they ought to see a feeling and kind friend, they behold only a detestable monster'. De Lacey tries to reassure him, offering to put his case to these people. He is overjoyed at such benevolence, but soon the rest of the family reappear; Agatha faints, Safie, for all her boldness, runs out without trying to assist her, and Felix belabours the monster with a stick. 'I could have torn him limb from limb, as the lion rends the antelope,' the monster recalls. 'But my heart sunk within me as with bitter sickness, and I refrained.' Faced with this evidence of the imperfection even of such upright seeming people – 'prejudice clouds their eyes' more effectively than De Lacey's actual blindness – the monster begins to despair of ever gaining acceptance. The idea of taking revenge on his 'cursed creator' begins to take hold of him; he kills William only because he discovers his identity – the luckless William proclaims, to this creature deprived of father, status, and name, 'My papa is a Syndic' (a senior state legislator), 'he is Monsieur Frankenstein – he would punish you'. The inevitable has happened: as Shelley's anonymous review, designed to promote the book in 1818 but not published until 1832, concludes, 'Treat a person ill, and he will become wicked. Requite affection with scorn; – let one being be selected, for whatever cause, as the refuse of his kind – divide him, a social being, from society, and you impose upon him the irresistible obligations – malevolence and selfishness'.

Many other elements went into the making of *Frankenstein*. In late July 1816, leaving the baby William with his Swiss nurse, Elise Duvillard, the Shelley group went on a six-day Alpine expedition which took them, by way of immense pines, waterfalls, and the rushing rivers Arve and Arvéron, to Chamonix and Mont Blanc. They were struck, on the mountain, by a sense of extraordinary vastness and desolation. 'The most desolate place in the world', Mary Godwin declared in the new journal begun for this trip, was the glacier known as the Mer de Glace. In this appropriately stark setting she chose to place the first confrontation between Frankenstein and his monster. Himself still 'troubled' two months after the death of Justine, Frankenstein picks his way across the uneven surface, 'rising like the waves of a troubled sea, descending low, and interspersed by rifts that sink deep'. Beneath 'the awful majesty of Mont Blanc', gazing back along the 'wonderful and stupendous scene' of the Sea of Ice, Frankenstein feels, briefly, 'something like joy'. But at once

Mary Shelley

a fierce reminder of sorrow intrudes on the scene: he sees 'the figure of a man ... advancing towards me with superhuman speed', unnaturally large, bounding over the ice where Frankenstein had trod with caution.

No doubt these icy wastes had some influence on the setting of the outer 'frame' of the novel. Here the narrator is Robert Walton, an English explorer whose ambition is to reach the North Pole. While writing the first draft of some of this material in the autumn of 1816 Mary Godwin read such relevant works as George Anson's *A Voyage Round the World*. In common with a number of the author's contemporaries, Walton has an optimistic notion that beyond the 'icy climes' of the north may lie a calm sea and 'a region of beauty and delight' from which 'snow and frost are banished'. In this wonderful place, he assures his sister – the recipient of his letters, seen by many as another marginalised female figure – 'I may ... discover the wondrous power which attracts the needle' and 'satiate my ardent curiosity', treading 'a land never before imprinted by the foot of man'. By finding the secret of the magnet and a passage to the wondrous pole he would, he goes on rather insistently, confer an 'inestimable benefit' on 'all mankind to the last generation'.

Ice closes round Walton's ship, stopping progress towards his goal, but he and his crew are distracted from their plight by the sight of a 'being which had the shape of a man, but apparently of gigantic stature' driving a dog-drawn sledge at speed across the 'vast and irregular plains of ice'. The ice around the ship breaks up soon afterwards and the crew take on board a man marooned on another sledge on a large block of ice: Frankenstein, who has pursued the monster to the frozen ends of the earth after the death of Elizabeth.

Walton soon comes to believe that in Frankenstein he has at last found the friend whose lack he once lamented. Frankenstein returns his warmth sufficiently to tell him his story – his own narrative and, within that, his creature's. The presence of these three different layers of narrative – Walton's, Frankenstein's, and the creature's – provides, in the structure of the novel, a powerful reminder of the importance of individual perspectives on, or constructions of, events; the short 1818 introduction and then the longer, more detailed 1831 account function as yet another layer. More immediately, the parallels between Walton's 'ardent curiosity' and his friend's soon become apparent. (Magnetism, like electricity, was widely regarded as a possible source of life.) Walton, to whose letters we return after Frankenstein has completed his narrative, is willing to risk anything to succeed in his quest. Frankenstein, the earlier overreacher, at first seems to encourage this attitude when he eloquently pleads with Walton's demoralised, depleted crew not to give up the chance of glory and go home. But in the end, as Frankenstein lies dying, by which time the men have decided that they will indeed insist on returning to England, he counsels Walton 'Seek happiness in tranquillity, and avoid ambition, even if it be only the apparently innocent one of distinguishing yourself in science and discoveries'. (Human or incorrigible, he does qualify this by adding 'I have myself been blasted in these hopes, yet another may succeed'.) More sharply, Frankenstein earlier refused to tell him how he made the creature – '"Are you mad, my friend, or whither does your senseless curiosity lead you?"' – and a minor addition of 1831 echoes this when Walton worries, trapped in the ice, that his crew will perish because of his own 'mad scheme'.

After Frankenstein's death, just at the point where, directed by Walton's friendship and affinity with him, our sympathies may be swinging back to the creator and his sufferings, the creature arrives and, in dialogue with Walton, reminds us of his own equally great sufferings. Again a different voice complicates our reactions, the more so because the monster shows considerable sympathy for Frankenstein. What is emphasised above all, as he mourns his creator and destroyer, is the lost potential for good of both creature and creator. Now all that is left is for the monster to seek peace in suicide. Mounting his ice-raft, 'he was soon borne away by the waves, and lost in darkness and distance'.

Bath, Marlow and London, 1816–18

At the end of August Shelley, Mary Godwin and Claire Clairmont set off for England. To avoid possible scandal it was desirable to remove Clairmont from Geneva and Byron before her pregnancy became generally apparent. Shelley, besides, had financial business to transact at home. In September the group settled in lodgings in the spa-town of Bath. They chose not to live in or close to London in order to keep the Godwins from finding out about Clairmont's pregnancy. 'Mrs Clairmont', as she called herself in Bath, gave birth to Allegra Byron in January 1817.

Mary Godwin was much occupied with the transformation of the original *Frankenstein* story or novella into the draft of a full-length book. Shelley, meanwhile, was often absent, in London or elsewhere, on financial or legal business or looking for new accommodation. She seized what opportunities she could to join him for a few days, but more often she was in Bath without him and, equally frustrating, with her stepsister. On 5th December 1816, when Shelley was in Marlow, near Windsor, staying with his friend Thomas Love Peacock and looking for a house, Mary wrote to him that the ideal place for them would be by a river or lake with 'noble trees and divine mountains' but she will happily make do with less – simply 'give me a garden and *absentia Clariae* and I will thank my love for many favours'. The desperation shows through the seemingly flippant use of Latin. Absence of Claire was difficult to achieve in view of the melancholy knowledge that Shelley wanted, and saw it as his duty, to do everything possible to help and protect her.

In October they had been reminded that there are worse fates than an excess of stepsister. Fanny Godwin, always depressive, her loyalties divided between the Godwins and the runaways, and her future uncertain, had travelled to Swansea and killed herself with an overdose of laudanum. Family members collaborated in drawing as little attention as possible to her death – one more potential scandal. Mary Godwin mourned sincerely but, it would seem, fairly briefly. Their relationship had never been particularly close. Another suicide, Harriet Shelley's, of which Shelley learnt on 15th December, excited rather less grief. He was shocked for a time but was soon claiming – improbably, most biographers feel – that she had drowned herself after the unhappy end of an affair with a certain groom called Smith.

In later, superstitious moments Mary Shelley imagined that misfortune had been visited on her because of Harriet's sad fate, but at the time she did not hesitate to take advantage of the situation by marrying Shelley. This would enable her to be reconciled at last with Godwin. For Shelley the marriage was particularly desirable since he seemed more likely to obtain custody of Ianthe and Charles, his children by Harriet, if he could provide a respectably married stepmother for them. Mary expressed eagerness to welcome the children into her home, but in March 1817 the Lord Chancellor refused Shelley custody on the grounds of the 'immoral opinions' and conduct he might be expected to inculcate. Ianthe and Charles were sent, after further legal battles, to live with foster parents.

For various practical reasons, then, 'the ceremony, so magical in its effects', as Shelley called it, took place at St Mildred's church, Bread Street, London on 30th December 1816. The main magical effect was the resumption of normal relations with the Godwins, who were present at the wedding. (They were still blissfully unaware of Clairmont's less happy situation.) Godwin's and Shelley's contact since 1814 had been almost entirely connected with money, and it continued to complicate their relationship now. Godwin was convinced that his son-in-law could raise more cash for him than he did, and was distinctly displeased if he heard that funds were being diverted elsewhere, principally to Shelley's new friend, the incurably impecunious poet and editor Leigh Hunt (1784–1859).

Mary Shelley saw much of Hunt and his wife Marianne when she came back to London from Bath at the end of January 1817, and for several weeks the Shelleys lived with them at their house in the Vale of Health, Hampstead. There was much socialising and theatre-going and debate. One night at the Hunts' they talked politics until three in the morning with William Hazlitt. They met the young poet John Keats. Mary was at last able to see her father often and to meet old friends like the Lambs at Skinner Street. And there was a splendid amount of '*absentia Clariae*': when Clairmont came to London on 18th February she took separate lodgings with her baby, Allegra.

From the Hunts' the Shelleys went, early in March, to Marlow. They stayed with Peacock and his mother before moving into the spacious Albion House, on which, optimistically, they took out a twenty-one-year lease. The house had an extensive garden. Nearby, as Mary Shelley remembered it later in her edition of Shelley's poetry, 'the chalk hills break into cliffs that overhang the Thames, or form valleys clothed with beech'. Less idyllically, most local people were underpaid, over-taxed, and suffering the after-effects of a bad harvest. Shelley's indignation at this

Albion House, Marlow, the Shelleys' home in 1817–18.

The British Library, London, Ashley MS B 3236 f.13

state of affairs prompted him, his wife recalled, both to financial generosity and to 'pleadings for the human race' in verse. In the house the Shelleys' favourite room was the library, which, Mary told Marianne Hunt, was 'a delightful place very fit for the luxurious literati'. In the library stood statues of Venus and Apollo, the gods of love and poetry; buying on credit, Shelley spared no expense to furnish the new home, a fact which must have been all too apparent to Godwin when he visited.

In Marlow Mary Shelley finished revising and fair-copying *Frankenstein*. John Murray, Byron's publisher, showed some interest in the novel but decided to reject it, as did two other publishers before it was accepted by the Lackington company, who specialised in books on ghosts and the occult, in September. Attending to the proofs was Mary Shelley's main literary activity that autumn, some weeks after she gave birth to a daughter, Clara, on 2nd September. Late in the pregnancy she had worked on the final version of the first half of the *History of a Six Weeks' Tour*, adapted from the 1814 journal, and in October she found time to finish work on the second half, comprising adaptations of two of her letters to Fanny, and Shelley's two Alpine letters to Peacock, from the summer of 1816. The whole work, her first in print, was published anonymously, by Thomas Hookham and Charles and James Ollier, on 6th November 1817.

Shelley, who was in London off and on for most of the autumn, forwarded proof revisions to Lackington. Shelley did not, as has sometimes been suggested, introduce substantial changes of his own. On the whole he confined himself to minor verbal alterations and corrections. Certainly he had taken a keen interest in the way the novel developed; equally, Mary Shelley was closely involved in his work. In December 1817, for example, she took part in discussions about how to tone down his *Laon and Cythna*, a long, pro-revolutionary poem in which the lovers are brother and sister. This had just been published and then rapidly withdrawn by the Olliers; the revision appeared as *The Revolt of Islam* in 1818. ('Work – walk – alterations for Cythna' she noted in the journal.) Frequently she copied poems by Shelley. Sometimes, as the 'Child of love and light' to whom *Laon* or *The Revolt* is dedicated, she inspired them.

Frankenstein was published on 1st January 1818. Again the work was anonymous, but its dedication to Godwin immediately announced the author's

Even like a bark which from a chasm of mountains
Dark vast & overhanging, on a river
Which there collects the strength of all its *fountains*
Comes forth, whilst with the speed its frame doth
Sails, oars & the arm tending to one endeavour *quiver*
So from that chasm of light a winged *form*
On all the ~~blast~~ *winds* of Heaven approaching *ever*
It ~~floated~~ — dilating as it came: the storm
Pursued it with fierce blast & lightnings swift
& warm.

A fragment of Percy Bysshe Shelley's fair copy of Laon and Cynthia.

The British Library, Ashley MS. A4048 f.115

political leanings. This was in itself a reason for the hostility of more conservative readers and reviewers. Reading the book confirmed their suspicions: the Godwinian sympathy for all those excluded by society soon became evident. The savage monster could easily be identified with 'the mob' and all its terrifying French-revolutionary associations. This was one of the unspoken reasons for the conclusion of John Wilson Croker, in the *Quarterly Review*, that *Frankenstein* is a 'tissue of horrible and disgusting absurdity. ... It inculcates no lesson of conduct, manners, or morality'. A number of reviews were, however, more discerning. The poet, novelist and editor Sir Walter Scott, writing in *Blackwood's Edinburgh Magazine*, detected some inexperience in the author but praised his – Shelley's, he believed – 'uncommon powers of poetic imagination' and felt it to be 'no slight merit ... that the tale, though wild in incident, is written in plain and forcible English'. Mary Shelley wrote to Scott in June to explain that she was the author of this 'juvenile attempt'. The first edition of the subsequently much sold 'attempt' raised £41.13s.10d. for the author: a third of the publisher's receipts after deduction of expenses.

On 9th February 1818 the group left Marlow for London, where they lived at 119 Great Russell Street for a month before setting out for Italy. They went for a variety of reasons. They wanted to see Byron, who had been living in Italy since the autumn of 1816, in the hope of forcing him to make a decision about Allegra's future. In the meantime the Shelleys had taken on the financial responsibility of looking after both Allegra and her mother. Another reason was Shelley's persistent ill-health. Although Dr William Lawrence had concluded, contrary to earlier diagnoses, that he did not have tuberculosis, he was still recommending a warmer climate. Life abroad, moreover, was less expensive – Shelley's debts amounted to £1,500 – and further from the reach of his creditors and the demanding Godwin. Finally, the Shelleys were aware of the real danger that if they stayed in England the courts, having refused him custody of the children of his first marriage, would remove William and Clara from the care of such alarmingly free-thinking parents.

'Sorrow's most obscure abode': Italy, 1818–19

The expedition began happily. There was sun, there were nostalgic views of Mont Blanc in the distance, stimulating political conversation with republicans in Lyon, fine white bread when they entered Italy, opera and ballet in Turin and at La Scala, Milan. Shelley's health, and everyone's spirits, improved in the southern spring warmth. (A less happy note was struck, occasionally, when the travellers saw examples of social oppression – a chain-gang in Pisa, for instance.) In May 1818 the party moved on to Livorno, where they met Maria Gisborne, an old friend of Mary Shelley's parents, who talked at length about her memories of Mary Wollstonecraft. They spent the summer at Bagni di Lucca, a Tuscan watering-place popular with English visitors, and enjoyed riding up through the chestnut woods to the Prato Fiorito or 'flowery meadow'.

In August a complex sequence of events was the beginning of the end of such carefree times. At the end of April Clairmont had agreed to send the fifteen-month-old Allegra, in the care of the Swiss nurse Elise Duvillard, to join Byron in Venice. But by August she was desperate to see her child. Shelley, hoping to gauge Byron's intentions, set off for Venice with her on 17th August. He went to see Byron alone, realising that he would be distinctly less amenable to any scheme for reuniting mother and daughter if he saw Clairmont or even knew that she was nearby. Since his brief affair with her Byron had been involved in many other liaisons and lesser encounters. The meeting between the two poets went well. They talked at Palazzo Mocenigo, rode on the Lido, and talked again at the palace. Their conversation and the landscape of Lido inspired one of Shelley's most readable poems, *Julian and Maddalo*. Byron's renewed interest in Shelley seemed also to promise hope for Clairmont since, to Shelley's surprise, he casually agreed that she could see Allegra. He offered the group the use of I Capuccini, the villa he was renting some miles inland at Este; Allegra could stay with them, for a time at least. Shelley's difficulty, however, was that he had told Byron that the women and children were in Padua, not far from Este. Rather than admit that this was a lie and jeopardise Byron's friendly mood, Shelley wrote at once to explain the situation to his wife and tell her to 'come instantly to Este'.

Driven by Paolo Foggi, who had recently entered the Shelleys' service, and accompanied by their servant from Marlow, Milly Shields, the mother and children set off from Bagni di Lucca as soon as they could. 'Sunday 30th. My Birthday – 21 – Packing', she noted tersely. After days of hot, dusty travelling, they reached Este on 5th September. I Capuccini was, she said later, 'cheerful and pleasant', but by the time they got there Clara, whose first birthday fell on the 2nd, had developed dysentery. Only three weeks later did her parents realise how ill she was. They took her to Venice, where they hoped to consult a good doctor, but she died in her mother's arms very soon after they reached the city. 'This is the Journal book of misfortunes', Mary Shelley headed her diary entry for that day.

Byron and the British consul and his wife, the Hoppners, did what they could to distract her from her grief. Somehow she toured the Venetian sights, using the fourth canto of Byron's *Childe Harold's Pilgrimage* as a poetical guide. Byron asked her to transcribe his more recent 'Ode on Venice' and his verse drama *Manfred*. Her close contact with him (without her stepsister) in September and October, added to her already deep interest in his work, seems to have given her something to cling to. Certainly it fuelled her exploration of various sorts of 'Byronic' character in several subsequent novels.

In Venice, however, she was evidently still in a state of shock after her daughter's death. The journey that almost certainly killed Clara had been in vain; Shelley failed to persuade Byron that Allegra could stay permanently with her mother. In late October Shelley collected the child from Este and brought her back to Byron in Venice. (Although Byron liked the Shelleys, he was not prepared, he told the Hoppners, to have Allegra 'perish of starvation, and green fruit' in their unconventional household, 'or be taught to believe that there is no Deity'.) And so, with only one child now – William, his parents' blue-eyed 'Willmouse' – the group set off on its travels once more.

They saw, as Mary Shelley notes in her journal, the 'armchair and inkstand' and manuscripts of the poet Ariosto in the library at Ferrara, the paintings of Guido Reni in Bologna, and 'the graceful dash of water' of the magnificent falls of Terni.

During their week in Rome they saw a great deal including St Peter's and, several times, the Colosseum, where they were keen to wander for themselves in the 'exhaustless mine/Of contemplation' of *Childe Harold*. Shelley then went ahead to look for accommodation in Naples. As the others, driven by Foggi, followed more slowly, they came to a plain 'covered with a wood of olives festooned by vines' and the supposed villa and tomb of Cicero, the Roman orator, politician and philosopher, on the bay of Gaeta. As Mary thought of Cicero the calm scene harmonised with her mood: 'The waves of the sea broke close under the windows of his villa which was perhaps then shaded as it is now by an olive grove and scented by orange and lemon trees'. He was killed by his enemies, she believed, in the wood, but the distance of the centuries and the peacefulness of the place removed the pain and, for a time at least, soothed her own grief.

In Naples the family lived at 250 Riviera di Chiaia, one of the busiest and most fashionable streets. They went to the many ancient sites around Vesuvius: to Pompeii

The ancient city of Pompeii, near Vesuvius. Excavation of the site began in 1748. Mary Shelley visited Pompeii in 1818, 1819 and 1843.

The British Library, London, 568.f.16

(where excavation had begun in 1748) several times; to 'Baiae's bay' where, in Shelley's 'Ode to the West Wind' (1819), 'The blue Mediterranean ... lay,/Lulled by the coil of his Crystalline streams'; to the cave of the Sibyl by Lake Averno, where Mary Shelley later set the introduction to *The Last Man*. She particularly liked to read the poems of Virgil in or near the sites traditionally associated with him; her favourite poem, she told Maria Gisborne, was Virgil's *Georgics*, and probably her careful reading of this rural poem, in the original Latin, went some way, like the groves near Gaeta, to further the calm she sought in the months after Clara's death.

There is a more mysterious side to the months in Naples. In February 1819 Shelley officially registered the birth of a child named Elena Adelaide Shelley. She was allegedly the Shelleys' daughter, born in December at 250 Riviera di Chiaia. Her identity remains a matter of speculation. Elise Duvillard, who had married Paolo Foggi at the time of his dismissal for cheating the Shelleys early in 1819, later told the Hoppners that the child was Shelley's and Claire Clairmont's. Probably this was the 'fact' Foggi threatened to reveal publicly in June 1820; the would-be blackmailer (or 'superlative rascal', as Mary Shelley described him to Gisborne) was successfully chased off by the Shelleys' Italian lawyer, but the following summer, while visiting Byron in Ravenna, Shelley discovered that the story was still circulating. The Hoppners had passed the gossip on to Byron. Shelley wrote at once to his wife, whose emphatic denial – 'Claire had no child [and so] the rest must be false' – is the most convincing evidence against the charge. But whose child was Elena? She may have been Elise's daughter by Shelley, Byron or someone else, Shelley's daughter by another woman, or, perhaps most likely, a Neapolitan orphan or foundling whom Shelley wanted to adopt. If so, Mary Shelley presumably objected to the idea; Elena was left behind in Naples when they moved on at the end of February 1819, although Shelley, apparently without his wife's knowledge, went on sending money for the child's maintenance until her death in June 1820.

In March they arrived back in Rome, where the low cost of accommodation compared with that in England again enabled them to live in pleasant locations, first at Palazzo Verospi on the Corso, the city's main fashionable thoroughfare, and then at 65 Via Sistina, another long, elegant street. For all the natural beauty of the Bay of Naples, Mary Shelley preferred Rome. 'Rome is formed by men,' she wrote to an acquaintance in 1820, '- a city in the midst of a desert, its associations and being are entirely human'. They repeatedly visited the Vatican Museum, Colosseum, Capitol and Pantheon, the whole 'wondrous city' in which the lonely Verney wanders at the end of *The Last Man*: a place 'hardly more illustrious for its heroes and sages, than for the power it exercised over the imaginations of men'. Here 'the meanest streets were strewed with truncated columns, broken capitals ... and sparkling fragments of granite or porphyry. ... The voice of dead time, in still vibrations, is breathed from these dumb things, animated and glorified as they were by man'.

It was probably in Rome in the spring of 1819 that Mary Shelley wrote her unfinished tale 'Valerius, the Reanimated Roman'. Valerius struggles to cope with the decay of his noble and powerful Rome and the city's take-over by 'superstitious' Catholicism. Only the splendour of the Colosseum and the friendship of a classically minded young Scotswoman afford him some comfort. The author gives no details of how the Roman was reanimated, but, as in *Frankenstein*, the focus is on the exclusion suffered by a creature of a different order – or at least, in Valerius' case, of a man from a different period and outlook.

Much of the time in Rome, however, Mary Shelley seems to have been happy not to write but to walk the sites, take drawing lessons, watch 'the important and foolish' English visitors in Holy Week, and enjoy the company of three-year-old William. She took him with her to places like the 'mountainous ruins of the Baths of Caracalla', where his father was working on his most notable longer work *Prometheus Unbound* amid, as his preface puts it, 'the flowery glades, and thickets of odoriferous blossoming trees, which are extended in ever winding labyrinths upon its immense platforms and dizzy arches suspended in the air'. William too was fascinated by ancient survivals, if on an appropriately smaller scale – he liked the statues, Mary Shelley wrote to Maria Gisborne, 'the goats and the horses and the men rotti' ('broken men', in his mixture of English and Italian) and 'the ladie's marbel feet'.

This happy interlude ended abruptly. William fell ill with worms, a fairly minor ailment, in late May. The Shelleys decided to move to somewhere cooler, probably back to Bagni di Lucca, to aid his recovery, but delayed too long. Like many people in Rome before the marshes of the surrounding Campagna were drained later in the century, he caught malaria. Within five days, in spite of the efforts of the

family's doctor in Rome, John Bell, William was dead. He was buried in the new Protestant cemetery, at this stage, according to Shelley, 'an open space among the ruins' (near one of the ancient city walls).

Mary Shelley expressed some of her feelings in a letter to Marianne Hunt three weeks later. They came to Italy for Shelley's health, and now the climate has killed their children. 'May you my dear Marianne never know what it is to lose two only and lovely children in one year – to watch their dying moments – and then at last to be left childless and for ever miserable'. She tries to talk about other things but the grief wells up again: 'William was so good so beautiful so entirely attached to me – To the last moment almost he was in such abounding health and spirits – and his malady appeared of so slight a nature.' In spite of this outpouring she found it difficult, from now on, to communicate her feelings to Shelley or to anyone else. The delayed shock of Clara's death less than a year earlier added to her grief for William. She was already given, like her mother and her sister Fanny, to periods of depression. Probably Godwin was less insensitive than fearful that she would kill herself when he wrote sternly counselling her to do her duty to society and not 'to think there is something fine, and beautiful, and delicate, in giving yourself up, and agreeing to be nothing'. Lines which Shelley wrote after they had moved to Villa Valsovano at Montenero, near Livorno, towards the end of June, show – more sensitively than her father's words, it is true – the situation as it seemed to him:

> *My dearest Mary, wherefore hast thou gone*
> *And left me in this dreary world alone?*
> *Thy form is here indeed – a lovely one –*
> *But thou art fled, gone down the dreary road,*
> *That leads to Sorrow's most obscure abode …*
> *For thine own sake I cannot follow thee,*
> *Do thou return for mine.*

But Mary Shelley did not quite give way to despair. She later observed in her journal that 'when I wrote *Matilda*, miserable as I was, the *inspiration* was sufficient to quell my wretchedness temporarily'. This therapeutic effect is the starting-point for the novella *The Fields of Fancy* – the first draft of *Matilda* – which she wrote in August and September 1819 at Villa Valsovano. The author or narrator has 'suffered a misfortune that reduced me to misery and despair', but as she sits crying she is visited by 'a lovely spirit whom I have ever worshipped and who tried to repay my adoration by diverting my mind from the hideous memories that racked it'. The spirit's name is Fantasia, related to the 'Fancy' or imagination of the title. Once, in

The beginning of The Fields of Fancy, *Mary Shelley's rough draft for her novel* Matilda.

Bodleian Library, Oxford, Dep.d.374/2

The Field of Fancy

It was in Rome — the Queen of the World that I suffered a misfortune that reduced me to misery & despair — The bright sun & azure sky were oppressive but nought was so hateful as the voice of man — I loved to walk by the shores of the Tiber which were solitary & if the sirocco blew to see the swift clouds pass over St. Peters and the many domes of Rome or if the sun shone I turned my eyes from the sky whose light was too dazzling & gay to be reflected in my tearful eyes I turned them to the river whose swift course was as the speedy departure of happiness and whose turbid colour was gloomy as grief —

Whether I slept I know not or whether it was in one of those many hour

evident allusion to *Frankenstein*, she led the author to a place 'whose grim terrors frighted sleep from the eye', but now 'you need more pleasing images'. She transports her to the 'pleasing' Elysian Fields, where a priestess, Diotima, is instructing people who were virtuous in life but whose suffering shut them out from the knowledge of love and beauty. Among Diotima's pupils is a young woman, Matilda, who now tells the story of the 'dark and phrenzied passions' which ruined her life.

Matilda's suffering comes about because her father falls incestuously in love with her. He has been absent for sixteen years following the death of her mother. He spends one rapturous year in Matilda's company before his jealousy, when a handsome young man pays her 'attentions', makes him realise the nature of his love. Overnight the father's manner changes. He frowns, shuns her, and and treats her either harshly or with 'a more heart-breaking coldness'. Months later he at last confesses to her the passion he has been trying to avoid. He leaves a letter saying that he will travel once more and never see her again; fearing the worst, she pursues him towards the sea but arrives too late to stop him from drowning himself. Subsequently, letting others suppose that she too has died, she goes off to live in a remote cottage on 'a dreary heath bestrewn with stones'. Here she is calm for a time but cannot escape from her sense of loss, despair, and pollution by 'the unnatural love I had inspired'.

Mary Shelley's strong and sometimes frustrated love for her own father may have influenced the choice of topic. But incest was, in any case, a common theme in literature of the time and, as Shelley told Maria Gisborne, 'like many other *incorrect* things a very poetical circumstance'. In the roofed and glazed terrace at the top of Villa Valsovano he was working on another tale of father/daughter incest, his verse play *The Cenci*. Mary Shelley copied it for him while she was working on *The Fields of Fancy*. In 1818 she had transcribed, and later translated, the play's main Italian source. Before undertaking it himself, in fact, Shelley had urged her to dramatise this tale in which the arrogant and cruel Count Cenci rapes his daughter, Beatrice, who then, with her mother's aid, kills him and is executed. Incest was now a suitably sombre theme for a writer in Mary Shelley's situation. It gave her the opportunity to explore the way in which, as Diotima says, 'the good and evil of the world' are 'inextricably intwined together': love ruins everything for Matilda and her father. It also allowed an interesting psychological focus on the heroine's sense of guilt, her sense that 'unlawful and detestable passion had poured its poison into my ears and changed all my blood' into 'a cold fountain of bitterness corrupted in its very source'. It is the unfair guilt of the bereaved, of the sexually abused; as in *Frankenstein* the victim is punished and excluded.

Later in the year Mary Shelley revised *The Fields* into *Matilda*. She sent it to Godwin in February 1820. His verdict was clear: although he liked parts of the work, the subject was 'disgusting and detestable; and there ought to be ... if [it] is ever published, a preface to prepare the minds of readers, and to prevent them from being tormented by the apprehension from moment to moment of the fall [the loss of virginity, in other words] of the heroine'. He approved of *The Cenci*, but there Beatrice hates her father throughout and distance is provided by the Renaissance setting, pseudo-Renaissance verse, and dramatic genre. *Matilda* sounds much more confessional, partly because the material involving Fantasia and Diotima had been excised during revision. It is this, probably much more than any personal sensitivity, which led Godwin not to seek publication for the work. It remained among his papers and was not published until 1959.

Godwin would have approved of the way his daughter worked to stave off despair. She was busy not only with *Matilda* but with initial transcripts and fair copies of her husband's poems. The couple's dedication to work surprised Sophia Stacey, a young relative of Shelley's on a visit to Florence, who recorded that 'He is always reading, and at night has a little table with pen and ink, she the same'. Shelley enjoyed Stacey's singing and addressed several poems to her, but Mary Shelley was not impressed: 'if she would learn the scales [she] would sing exceedingly well,' she wrote to Maria Gisborne, and to the girl herself she made a slightly barbed remark about how little 'many of our English Butterflies' see of Italy.

One of the sights Shelley proudly displayed to his visitor was his new son. Percy Florence, the Shelleys' only child to survive infancy, was born in Florence on 12th November 1819. (Sophia Stacey suggested the middle name.) Although he could not replace William and Clara, he gave his mother something to live for. The day after the baby's birth Shelley wrote to Leigh Hunt that 'Poor Mary begins (for the first time) to look a little consoled'.

～ *Pisa, San Terenzo and Genoa, 1820–23*

The three Shelleys moved with Claire Clairmont to Pisa in January 1820, lived in the Gisbornes' house in Livorno in June and July, and then moved to Bagni di San Giuliano, a few miles from Pisa, in August. In Pisa Mary Shelley wrote *Proserpine* and *Midas*, two short dramas based on myths from Ovid's *Metamorphoses*, and aimed at young readers. The work was partly collaborative: Shelley contributed several songs and dialogues. After several attempts she finally succeeded in publishing an abridged version of *Proserpine*, for a mainly adult audience, in *The Winter's Wreath for 1832*. She failed to place *Midas*, which remained unpublished until 1922, and was similarly unlucky with the story 'Maurice, or the Fisher's Cot', which she wrote at Bagni di San Giuliano soon after arriving there.

The opening of Mary Shelley's mythological drama Proserpine, *published in* The Winter's Wreath for 1832.

The British Library, London, pp6805

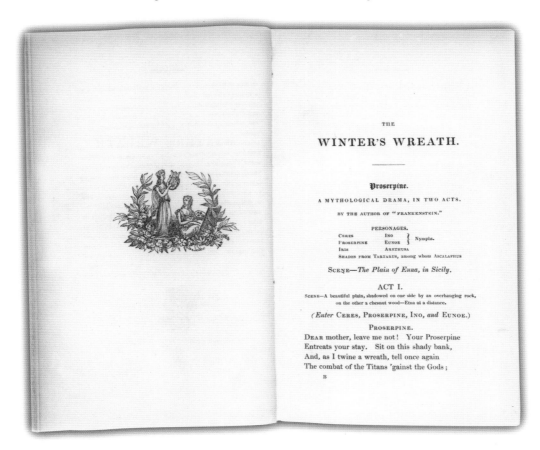

'Maurice' was also intended for a juvenile audience, at first a very specific one: Laurette, the eleven-year-old daughter of Margaret, formerly Lady Mountcashell, an Irishwoman whom the Shelleys had met on a visit to Pisa in September 1819. Mary Wollstonecraft had for a time been Margaret's governess; Wollstonecraft's *Original Stories* had been inspired by her experiences teaching her and her sister. The former pupil went on to write her own books for children and, partly under the influence of Wollstonecraft's ideas, left her husband, the Earl of Mountcashell, and came to live in Italy with her lover George Tighe. She had taken the name 'Mrs Mason', after the wise teacher who tells the *Original Stories*. 'Maurice' is the story of a boy who is stolen from his parents, suffers various hardships, remains kind and tolerant, and is eventually reunited with his father. (Lost children – her own and Allegra, kept away from her mother – were of course on the author's mind.) The story would probably attract little attention but for its extraordinary history. It was assumed to be lost until Laurette's manuscript was identified at the house of her sister's descendants in Italy in 1997 and published in 1998.

At Pisa Mary Shelley had embarked on a much more substantial piece of writing, a novel – later published as *Valperga* – about Castruccio Castracani, ruler of Lucca and other towns in Tuscany in the early fourteenth century. The primary reason for choosing to write a historical novel was Sir Walter Scott's great contemporary success in the genre. At an early stage of work on Castruccio a long-awaited box arrived from the Hunts, containing, in addition to clothes for the baby, three of Scott's novels, including his recent *Ivanhoe*. The box came on 7th June, the first anniversary of William's death; probably trying to distract herself from the date, she devoured all three books over the next few days. Extensive preparation also included visiting Castruccio sites in Lucca and reading Dante, various Italian chronicles, and Machiavelli's short *Vita di Castruccio Castracani*.

But contemporary as much as historical concerns are reflected in the struggle between the ruthless tyrant Castruccio and Euthanasia, the central female figure in *Valperga*, who supports the republic of Florence against him and whose Greek name – 'noble death' or 'good death' – stresses her commitment to principle. As far as the Shelleys and like-minded people were concerned, a similar battle was being fought in England, where on 16th August 1819, for example, soldiers had broken up a peaceful parliamentary reform meeting at St Peter's Fields in Manchester. Eleven people were killed and several hundred injured in the resulting 'Peterloo' massacre – named by analogy with Waterloo. In September Mary Shelley had made a press transcript of Shelley's vigorous poetic response to news of Peterloo, 'The Mask of Anarchy', which called on the people to

Percy Bysshe Shelley's autograph draft of 'The Mask of Anarchy'.

The British Library, Ashley MS 4086

> *Rise like Lions after slumber*
> *In unvanquishable number –*
> *Shake your chains to earth like dew*
> *Which in sleep had fallen on you –*
> *Ye are many – they are few.*

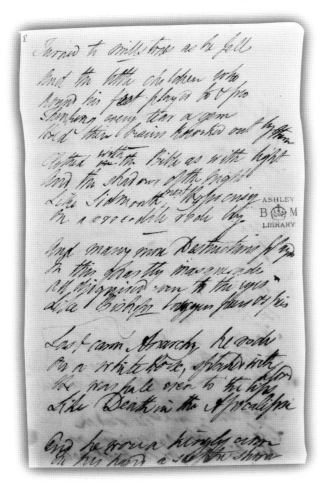

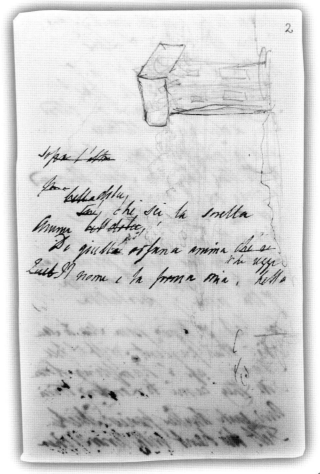

Events in other regions of Europe are also relevant to *Valperga*. Euthanasia dreams of the day when Italy might be free rather than, as it still was in the early nineteenth century, divided up between various absolutist and foreign or foreign-backed powers. In 1820 there were attempted republican revolutions in Naples and Piedmont. The memory of an earlier nationalist rising was kept alive in conversations at Mrs Mason's house in Pisa; she was related to Lord Edward Fitzgerald, the Irish rebel leader of 1798, and had sympathised with his cause. And towards the end of 1820 Mary Shelley became intimate with Prince Alexandros Mavrokordatos, an exile soon to become famous as a leader in the Greek war for independence from the Turkish Empire.

Castruccio himself is of more than simply medieval interest; 'he was,' Shelley told his publisher Charles Ollier, 'a little Napoleon, and, with a dukedom instead of an empire for his theatre, brought upon the same all the passions and errors of his antitype'. (Although Napoleon was sometimes regarded in a heroic light by liberal English writers, here he figures as the enemy of republican liberty.) There is, however, as much psychological as political interest in *Valperga*. The tyrant himself is originally a victim, if on a lesser scale than Frankenstein's creature, who turns aggressor – his family were banished from Lucca. His love for the pure, intelligent and peace-loving Euthanasia softens him at times, but his lust for power is stronger. Eventually, reluctantly, she decides that she cannot marry him. He subjugates her town and citadel of Valperga, where once her father had sheltered him. He tortures, kills or banishes many of her allies and followers. He finally avoids further

VALPERGA:

OR, THE

LIFE AND ADVENTURES

OF

CASTRUCCIO,

PRINCE OF LUCCA.

BY THE AUTHOR OF "FRANKENSTEIN."

IN THREE VOLUMES.
VOL. I.

LONDON:
PRINTED FOR G. AND W. B. WHITTAKER,
AVE-MARIA-LANE.

1823.

awkward reminders of his capacity for human feeling by exiling Euthanasia herself. He does earlier feel a twinge of guilt at the death of Beatrice, the other main female character, which results indirectly from her desperate state of mind after he thoughtlessly allows her to seduce him; but he assuages his guilt quite easily by bestowing on her a magnificent funeral.

Mary Shelley's progress on the novel was gradual. She was hampered by an eye inflammation, worry over Godwin's still disastrous finances, and a flooding canal which forced the Shelleys to move back from the Bagni to Pisa in October 1820.

A scene at Lucca by Henry Herbert Bullman. Castruccio Castracani, who figures in Mary Shelley's novel Valperga, *ruled Lucca in the early fourteenth century.*

But eventually in the autumn of 1821 she finished copying and revising the final draft and revisions. Charles Ollier refused the book, at this stage called *Castruccio, Prince of Lucca*, in spite of Shelley's persuasions. In London Godwin undertook to find another publisher. He introduced some alterations to help achieve this aim, changing the title to *Valperga: or, the Life and Adventures of Castruccio, Prince of Lucca* and removing details of battles which occurred towards the end of the already fairly lengthy narrative. Thus slightly reshaped, *Valperga* was published by G. and W.B. Whittaker in February 1823. It did not sell particularly well, partly perhaps because, in spite of Godwin's cuts, there was still too much of the archaeological element about which Shelley had enthused to Ollier: 'All the manners, customs, opinions, of the age are introduced; the superstitions, the heresies, and the religious opinions are displayed; the minutest circumstance of Italian manners in that age is not omitted'. Readers appreciated such minute detail when it was part of Scott's medieval England or seventeenth-century Scotland, but were apparently less enthusiastic about the details and complexities of life in Castruccio's Tuscany. Gender also affected this sort of response: politics, conventional wisdom had it, was no concern for a female author, and the *Literary Gazette* felt, with reference to Euthanasia, that 'it scarcely seems in woman's nature for patriotism to be a stronger feeling than love'.

Having moved back to Pisa after the flood, the Shelleys became more involved in the city's social life, and maintained links with it when they returned to the Bagni between May and October 1821. As well as the Greek exile Mavrokordatos they knew the learned physician Andrea Vaccà and the more enigmatic, eloquent and unreliable Francesco Pacchiani, a professor at the university whom some scholars have claimed as an inspiration for the sinister Battista Tripalda in *Valperga*. But the Shelleys' closest friends in Pisa as soon as they met them in January 1821 were Edward and Jane Williams. Much of the expatriate community was not willing to receive the Shelleys because of their unconventional past and rumours about atheism and Harriet's suicide. But the Williamses, who were not legally married, were in a similar position to the Shelleys. Edward Williams and Shelley went boating on canals and rivers, Mary Shelley read *Matilda* to the Williamses, and the whole group went on expeditions into the hills together.

There were also visits to Teresa Viviani, the daughter of the city governor, at the convent of Sant'Anna. At first both Shelleys were convinced that 'Emilia' (the more poetic name by which they decided to call her) was in effect a prisoner, about to be forced into an arranged marriage by her father and – exciting Mary Shelley's particular sympathy and recognition – wicked stepmother. But she soon realised that Viviani was not especially unhappy; as her wedding date approached she distanced herself from the Shelleys. Shelley, however, was much taken with her and addressed to her his poem *Epipsychidion*. This poem clearly should not be interpreted as simply an autobiographical document, but if Mary Shelley read it as such then she must have received the hurtful message that she, responsible for their 'chaste cold bed', had been replaced by a new object of desire. Unusually, he did not show her the poem for some time after writing it. On the other hand he once assured the girl that Mary Shelley's apparent coldness was 'only the ash which covers an affectionate heart'. Viviani was a subject of more passing interest, to be ranked with the many other schemes, ideals and people he passionately but briefly took up.

His relationship with Claire Clairmont was more permanent and more troublesome for Mary Shelley. Rivalry between two very different women for the love of a man is a traditional literary motif, but the presentation of Beatrice in *Valperga* is somewhat influenced by Clairmont; Beatrice even looks like her, with 'her deep black eyes, ... her curved lips, and face formed in a perfect oval'. Mary Shelley seems not, however, consciously to have defined her feelings about her stepsister as sexual jealousy. Both Shelleys pitied her for her separation from Allegra; Byron failed even to send news of the child. Shelley saw Clairmont as his pupil, as a brilliant but unstable person who needed his help. He also valued her companionship when his wife's heart was covered by the 'ash' of her mourning. But the daily friction became so great in the summer of 1821 that Clairmont agreed to live separately for a time at least. Another reason for her going was that her continued residence in what looked like a *ménage à trois* would make it difficult to pursue the career as a governess which she was considering. (This was almost the only option available to a highly educated single woman without much money.) After periods at the Gisbornes' house and with Mrs Mason she went to live as a paying guest with a family in Florence.

Following pages:

Pisa and the river Arno,1855, by David Roberts. The Shelleys lived in or near the city between January 1820 and April 1822.

Bridgeman Art Library

The Shelleys' social life entered a new phase with the arrival of Byron in Pisa on 1st November 1821. He had been preceded by Countess Teresa Guiccioli, with whom he had settled into an unusually stable relationship in 1819. The Shelleys had found Byron a house, Palazzo Lanfranchi (now Palazzo Toscanelli) on the river Arno, and had themselves moved back into the city, to rooms in the group of buildings known as the Tre Palazzi di Chiesa, on the other bank of the river. Over the next few months Shelley and Edward Williams spent much time riding, shooting, and talking with Byron and other male friends. Mary Shelley and Jane Williams saw less of Byron. Mary read and sometimes copied recent work for him, finding in his *Cain* 'the highest style of imaginative poetry'. But about Byron himself she remained, like her husband, somewhat ambivalent; Shelley, as at Lake Léman in 1816, felt inhibited in his own writing by Byron's fame and facility of composition, and his treatment of Clairmont and Allegra continued to rankle.

Mary Shelley developed a more satisfying relationship, from January 1822, with Edward John Trelawny, who had been invited to Pisa by his friend Edward Williams. Trelawny was an extraordinary, colourful figure, an ex-seaman and skilful teller of (often tall) stories. In her journal she recorded her first impressions of his 'abrupt, but not unpolished manners' and striking 'Moorish' features after talking to him at the opera:

*Edward John Trelawny,
by Edward Duppa.
Mary Shelley met
Trelawny, ex-seaman
and adventurer, in 1822.*

*National Portrait Gallery,
London*

*There is an air of extreme good nature which pervades his whole
countenance, especially when he smiles, which assures me that his heart is
good. He tells strange stories of himself – horrific ones – so that they harrow
one up, while with his emphatic but unmodulated voice – his simple yet
strong language – he portrays the most frightful situations. ... I believe them
now I see the man.*

She was at last excited about, half ready to be in love with, a new friend: 'tired with
the everyday sleepiness of human intercourse I am glad to meet with one who
among other valuable qualities has the rare merit of interesting my imagination'.

With Jane Williams, she saw much of Trelawny in the first few months of 1822. They were part of groups on country excursions, at the theatre, at the masked ball where Mary Shelley wore Turkish dress and Jane Williams 'Hindoostani'. Altogether Mary Shelley was happier here than she had been for a considerable period. The earlier coldness between her and her husband seemed to be over or at least less evident. By the end of March she knew that she was pregnant by Shelley for the fifth time.

The Shelleys and Williamses started looking for somewhere new to live in April; Clairmont had come on a visit to Pisa and went with the Williamses on an unsuccessful househunting trip to La Spezia. While they were away news reached Pisa that the five-year-old Allegra had died of typhus, at the convent to which her father had consigned her, on 20th April. On Clairmont's return to Pisa the Shelleys, deciding not to tell her until she was well away from Byron, took her as soon as possible back to La Spezia and then on to the only suitable accommodation they could find, the remote Villa Magni at San Terenzo, near Lerici. Here on 2nd May they broke the news. Clairmont reacted more calmly than expected, but never completely recovered from her loss and remained angry that others did not hate Byron as she did.

Villa Magni was the least happy of Mary Shelley's homes. The setting was bleak: the house stood alone and gave straight onto the sea; years later she recalled that when they first arrived 'the howling wind swept round our exposed house, and the sea roared intermittently'; what food they could obtain had to be brought from a village three miles away and across 'the torrent of the Magra'. In good weather the bay could be attractive, and in other circumstances she would have admired it; Shelley loved it, wrote productively, and was often out on the water with Williams in their new open sailing-boat. But Mary Shelley was suffering the strain of a difficult pregnancy and the death of Allegra, terrible in itself and also a reminder of the earlier deaths. To make matters worse the Williamses, having failed to find a satisfactory place of their own, were living with the Shelleys in an intimacy which sometimes verged on claustrophobia. Clairmont was also there except for two weeks at the end of May and beginning of June. Altogether, she remembered that in August, her 'nerves were wound up to the utmost irritation, and the sense of misfortune hung over my spirits'. She felt later, in her 'Note on Poems of 1822', that 'an intense

presentiment of coming evil brooded over my mind, and covered this beautiful place and genial summer with the shadow of coming misery'.

Communication between the Shelleys again all but ceased. There were fragments of their old closeness; 'her only moments of peace,' she told Gisborne, were on the boat, 'when lying down with my head on his knee I shut my eyes and felt the wind and our swift motion alone'. Shelley, however, was finding some of his 'moments of peace' in the easier company of Jane Williams. He enjoyed her singing, as he had always enjoyed Claire Clairmont's. So that she could accompany herself he bought her, in Pisa not long before they left, a magnificent mahogany and pine guitar (now, with its close-fitting wooden box, in the possession of the Bodleian Library in Oxford). He presented it to her with a poem. As with Emilia Viviani, he probably had little real intention of putting poetic words into adulterous practice. But Shelley needed the relationship, the communication; he confided in the Gisbornes that all he lacked in Italy was 'those who can feel, and understand me. Whether from proximity and the continuity of domestic intercourse, Mary does not'.

The stress that Shelley himself experienced at Villa Magni, for reasons doubtless including the impasse in his relationship with his wife, manifested itself in sleepwalking, nightmares and hallucinations. On the night of 23rd June he dreamt

Villa Magni and the boat that Byron wanted to call Don Juan *after his own poem. The Shelleys preferred* Ariel. *An illustration from Edward John Trelawny's* Recollections of the Last Days of Shelley and Byron *(1858).*

that the Williamses, bloodstained, pale, 'their bones starting through their skin', had come to warn him that the sea was flooding into the house. Next, Mary Shelley reports, he dreamt that 'he saw the figure of himself strangling' her. This scene probably reflected recent traumas. It may also have been related to the fact that he had saved her life only a week earlier. She had miscarried and, far from medical aid, lost a great deal of blood: 'for seven hours,' she told Gisborne, 'I lay nearly lifeless – kept from fainting by brandy, vinegar, eau de Cologne etc. – at length ice was brought to our solitude – it came before the doctor so Claire and Jane were afraid of using it but Shelley overruled them and by an unsparing application of it I was restored'. (He made her sit in a bath filled with the ice.)

Less than three weeks later Shelley and Edward Williams sailed their boat to Livorno to meet Leigh Hunt, who, after many delays, had arrived in Italy with his family. He was to be involved in writing for a new magazine, *The Liberal*, which would be made financially viable by the inclusion of work by the much better-known Byron. Shelley provided encouragement; in Pisa he persuaded Byron to bring out his satire *The Vision of Judgement* in the first number of *The Liberal*. Pleased at his success, Shelley went back to Livorno and on the early afternoon of 8th July 1822 he, Williams and the boat-boy, Charles Vivian, set off for home. Several hours later a great squall blew up and all three were drowned when their boat went down in the Gulf of Spezia.

The first indication that something was badly wrong reached Mary Shelley and Jane Williams on 12th, when a letter from Hunt arrived in which he asked for confirmation that the boat had returned safely in spite of the storm. A period of terrible uncertainty followed. The two women travelled fruitlessly to Pisa and Livorno in search of news. Mary reached Pisa, Byron and Guiccioli said, looking 'more like a ghost than a woman – light seemed to emanate from [her] features'. They tried to go on hoping until, on 19th, Trelawny came to tell them that the bodies had been washed ashore. Mary Shelley remembered that 'he did not attempt to console me, that would have been too cruelly useless; but he launched forth into as it were an overflowing and eloquent praise of my divine Shelley'. In August Trelawny also took charge of the cremations on the two beaches where the bodies had been temporarily buried in accordance with local health regulations. The widows did not attend; Mary Shelley was shown the box containing Shelley's ashes, which was later sent to Rome for burial beside his son William in the Protestant cemetery. (Unfortunately, however, the exact location of William's grave was no longer known.)

Mary Shelley's grief was intensified by remorse for her apparent coldness to Shelley in recent years. In October she began a new 'Journal of Sorrow' – 'white pages which I am to blot with dark imagery'. Often before this the journals had consisted mainly of lists of books read and people seen, but now she wrote compulsively, trying to re-establish communication:

> *Alas! I am alone – no eye answers mine – my voice can with none assume its natural modulation, all is show – and I but a shadow – What a change! Oh my beloved Shelley – It is not true that this heart was cold to thee. Tell me, for now you know all things – did I not in the deepest solitude of thought repeat to myself my good fortune in possessing you? How often during those happy days, happy though chequered, I thought how superiorly gifted I had been in being united to one to whom I could unveil myself, and who could understand me.*

She told herself in the journal, and others in letters, that he was an elemental being 'and that death does not apply to him', that his spirit now informed the nature he had loved. He would somehow guide her until they were reunited. (While not conventionally religious she had never entirely shared his atheism.) The mission she conceived, almost immediately after his death, of editing his work and writing his biography, was partly a way of expiating guilt, partly a way of sharing a version of her mythical creation, the 'divine Shelley', with an ignorant or misunderstanding public. Literary work gave, besides, a sense of purpose (and the possibility of earning urgently needed money). Even the simpler exercise of writing her journal, late at night, became especially important to her when the Hunts arrived to share with her Casa Negroto, a large house in Albaro, now part of Genoa. Leigh was sometimes querulous, Marianne ill, their many children often wild and uproarious. Claire Clairmont had gone to Vienna to join her brother Charles and from there went on to Russia as a governess in 1824. Jane Williams and her children had gone back to England in September.

Fighting depression, she began to gather Shelley's manuscripts. She copied several of the poems for inclusion in Hunt's *The Liberal*, which also published two of

her own essays and her story 'A Tale of the Passions; or the Death of Despina' in 1823. She was much occupied, too, in copying for Byron, who was also living in Albaro at Casa Saluzzo. She worked mainly on his wide ranging satirical poem *Don Juan*. Her dedication to work, together with her generally quiet and occasionally irritable manner, gave some of her friends the impression that she was less devastated by her loss than the obviously distraught Jane Williams. It was Jane herself who told Leigh Hunt, before she left Italy, that the Shelleys' marriage had been unhappy and left him in no doubt that the fault was the wife's. It seems that Leigh or Marianne Hunt made some allusion to this in November 1822, when Mary Shelley reflected bitterly in the diary on the hot tears which the emotions of her allegedly cold heart force her to shed. Reconciliation with Hunt came in June 1823, when he wrote to his friend the musician Vincent Novello, reporting his new understanding that 'she is a torrent of fire under ... snow' – much as Shelley had described her to Emilia Viviani – and 'had excuses of suffering little known to anybody but herself'.

There were difficulties, too, in Mary Shelley's relationship with Byron. His 'mere presence and voice' had a powerful effect on her. She told herself, in the journal, that this was because whenever he spoke she expected to hear Shelley answer, but she also clearly found him attractive. As Shelley's executor (Peacock, in England, was the other) he also had some reponsibility for her more practical interests. It fell to him, for instance, to ask Sir Timothy Shelley what provision he intended to make for his son's widow and his grandson, and to communicate to her the displeasing answer that since she had done much, in her father-in-law's opinion, to alienate Shelley from his family and duties, 'I must ... decline all interference in matters in which Mrs Shelley is interested'. Worse, Sir Timothy was prepared to help the child only 'if he shall be placed with a person I approve' in England. One of her disagreements with Byron happened because he advised her to accept this proposal; as his treatment of Allegra had suggested, he was unlikely to sympathise with her desire to have Percy 'perpetually with me – watching the dawnings of his mind, inspiring him with due respect for his unequalled father, and spreading joy over his infant years'.

A more complicated awkwardness developed in June 1823 after Mary Shelley had decided that returning to England would give her and her child a better chance of winning Sir Timothy's compassion. Byron had earlier promised to pay their fare, but she refused

Ah! he is gone – and I alone;
    How dark and dreary seems the time!
'Tis thus when the glad sun is flown,
    Night rushes o'er the Indian clime.

Is there no star to cheer this night –
    No soothing twilight for the heart?
Yes – memory sheds her fairy light,
    Beaming as sunsets golden hues.

And hope of dawn – Oh brighter far
    Thou clouds that in the orient burn,
More welcome than the morning star;
    Is the dear thought – he will return!

                    Mary W. Shelley

to let him because Hunt for some reason showed her letters in which Byron spoke 'with contempt against me and my lost Shelley'. Elsewhere Byron often spoke well of Shelley, and Hunt's subsequent conduct suggests that he may have encouraged her to take these derogatory remarks as seriously as possible. Byron, unaware of the reason for her sudden dislike, now tried secretly to provide the money through Hunt. But Hunt, often adept at acquiring other people's cash, simply pocketed it. Byron, with Trelawny, sailed to join the Greek fight for independence on 17th July 1823. Mary and Percy Florence Shelley set off for England, with the help of loans from Trelawny and Mrs Mason, eight days later.

〰 Presumption *and* The Last Man, *1823–26*

M ary Shelley faced the prospect of England – bad weather, social notoriety, money problems – with reluctance. But she was delighted to have arrived in time to see the popular dramatisation of her novel: *Presumption; or, the Fate of Frankenstein.*

She saw *Presumption* at the English Opera House (or Lyceum Theatre), with her father, her brother William, and Jane Williams, on 29th August 1823. This loose version of the novel, by Richard Brinsley Peake, uses some of the original characters and language, but adapts them freely to the theatrical conventions of the day: there are songs including a love duet for Felix and Safie, a dance of villagers, much racing around by Frankenstein with his pistol, and a spectacular conclusion in which creator and creature are both swallowed up by an avalanche. The hero, who becomes more alchemist than scientist, has a comic assistant called Fritz who, jumpy from the beginning, is terrified by his first sight of 'a hob – hob-goblin, seven-and-twenty feet high!' His master's reaction is also unambiguous: he at once condemns himself, in clear religious terms, as a miserable being whose 'impious labour' has 'presumptuously bestowed' the spark of life.

Peake's monster is not completely unsympathetic, but he too becomes a much simpler character – he cannot speak, let alone give Frankenstein or the blind De Lacey a civilised account of himself. The impact of this creature, as played by Thomas Potter Cooke with, the stage directions record, 'dark black flowing hair' and bluish skin (suggested by 'a light blue or French grey cotton dress, fitting quite close') was emphatically visual and his first appearance one of the highlights of the production. The play-bill whetted expectations, as Mary Shelley explained to Leigh Hunt: 'in the list of dramatis personae came, —— by Mr T. Cooke: this nameless mode of naming the unnameable is rather good'. Although 'the story is not well managed', Cooke 'played ——'s part extremely well – his seeking as it were for support – his trying to grasp at the sounds he heard – all indeed he does was well imagined and executed. I was much amused, and it appeared to excite a breathless eagerness in the audience'.

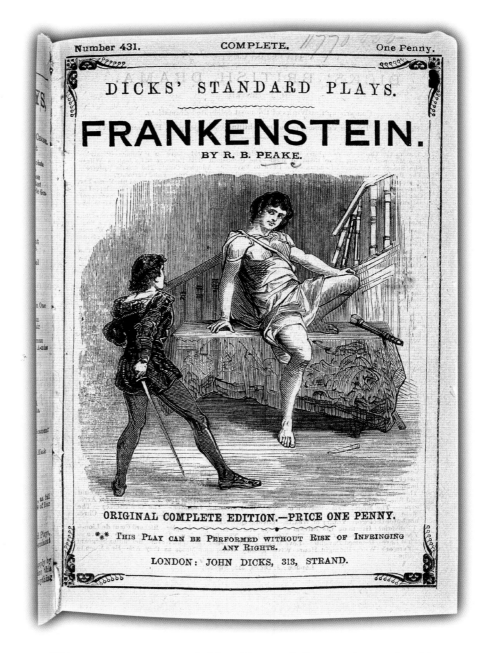

This eagerness was remarkably widespread. *Presumption* ran for thirty-seven performances at the English Opera House that summer, returned for a second run in 1824 and was often revived over the next twenty years. It spawned several similar pieces, the most spectacular of which was *Le Monstre et le magicien*, a longer play again featuring Cooke as the monster, which ran in Paris for some ninety-four performances in 1826. Later productions of *Presumption* replaced the climactic avalanche with the ending made popular by *Le Monstre* and its English version, where amid thunder and fire 'the Magician and his unhallowed abortion are with the boat engulfed in the waves'. In making this substitution producers were possibly mindful of the farcical Birmingham production of 1824 in which a whitewashed canvas elephant – a makeshift avalanche – was released prematurely, demolished the scenery, and came to rest on the footlights before, as the actor playing the monster recalled, 'the curtain dropped upon Frankenstein amid the laughter and applause of a good natured audience'.

The Royal Coburg Theatre in 1819. Henry Milner's The Man and the Monster; or, the Fate of Frankenstein *played here in July 1827.*

Enthoven Collection, Victoria and Albert Museum, London

Even before this débâcle, theatre managements had been well aware of the comic potential of the story, at least as told by Peake. Peake burlesqued his own play in *Another Piece of Presumption* for the Adelphi Theatre in October 1823. Here Frankinstitch, a tailor who has done 'such a damn'd deal of thinking lately' that his 'eyes and eyelashes look like red hairy gooseberries', makes a 'hobgoblin' from parts of nine of his colleagues. Endowed with Billy Burrows' head he can, unlike Peake's first monster, speak. As he and his creator expire, not only shot but deluged with cabbages and cauliflowers, he tries to find 'avalanche' in the dictionary which Frankinstitch gave him – the poor equivalent of the original Plutarch and Milton.

Other melodramas and burlesques were plentiful, among them *Humgumption; or, Dr Frankenstein and the Hobgoblin of Hoxton* (1823); *Frankenstein; or, the Demon of Switzerland* (1823) and *The Man and the Monster; or, the Fate of Frankenstein* (1826), both by Henry M. Milner; and *Frank-in-Steam, or, the Modern Promise to Pay* (1824; the sub-title alludes to that of the novel, *The Modern Prometheus*). A later comic offering, for Christmas 1849, was William and Robert Brough's *Frankenstein; or, the Model Man*. Some of these plays were performed regularly until at least the 1850s and they, probably more than the novel itself, made almost universally familiar the name 'Frankenstein', which, even at this stage, was often used to refer to the monster.

This scene from Frankenstein; or, the Model Man *appeared in the* Illustrated London News, *January 1850. The play ran for fifty-four performances at the Adelphi Theatre in 1849–50.*

The British Library, London, pp7611

Rightly or wrongly named, he began to appear in a range of non-literary contexts. The foreign secretary, George Canning, told the House of Commons in March 1824 that freeing slaves in the Caribbean would be like raising up an uncontrollable creature, 'with all the corporeal capabilities of man' but unable to tell right from wrong, 'resembling the splendid fiction of a recent romance'. Although Mary Shelley was grateful for the mention, Canning's moral was markedly different from hers. For her, slaves, like excluded monsters or women, were the badge of a distinctly unjust society. But the simplified monster of the theatre, politics, or casual conversation lent himself more easily to fear of mob rule on the French revolutionary model than to the reformist beliefs of the Godwin and Shelley circle. And so in the 1820s and early 1830s proponents of electoral reform were often depicted as Frankensteins raising up uncontrollable monsters, and Victorian caricatures show a variety of gigantic, hideous and threatening enemies of the British establishment, with titles like 'The Russian Frankenstein and his Monster'.

In these versions, Mary Shelley's creature is demonised as if Frankenstein or Felix has seized control of the tale. But even travesties of her story helped to keep it before the public. It was on the strength of the likely success of *Presumption* that Godwin arranged publication of a second edition of *Frankenstein* while his daughter was still on her way

This cartoon, 'The Russian Frankenstein and his Monster', appeared in Punch, *15 July 1854. The cartoon blames Russia for unleashing the devastation of the Crimean War.*

The British Library, London, pp5270

from Italy. This time her name appeared on the title-page. It would keep the Shelley name familiar, perhaps obtaining work for her and also preparing the way for her edition of Shelley's *Posthumous Poems* (1824). This selection of the less controversial of his poems began the long process by which his widow presented him to readers less as atheist and radical thinker than as visionary and lyric poet. The long-term project was hampered, however, by Sir Timothy Shelley. No legal settlement had been agreed, but he had reluctantly disbursed £100 for her and promised £100 a year for Percy. He now told her that if she wanted 'a sufficiency' from him she must withdraw the edition and refrain from further blackening of the family name. Needing money and not expecting her elderly father-in-law to live much longer, she agreed. (309 of the 500 copies of *Posthumous Poems* had already been sold, however.)

She abandoned plans to write Shelley's biography and delayed further editorial work on his poems, but was able to go on publishing her own books, short stories, and essays as 'the Author of *Frankenstein*'. This may well in fact have attracted more readers, while technically observing Sir Timothy's regulations. But it was only after much persistence – many visits and letters to Sir Timothy's solicitor –

The constant lovers Rosina and Flora, in Mary Shelley's tales 'The Invisible Girl' and 'The Brother and the Sister', both published in The Keepsake for 1833.

The British Library, London, pp6670

that she obtained a settlement and occasional grudging increases. Her father-in-law did show more interest in Percy once he became heir to the baronetcy on the death of his half-brother Charles (Shelley's son by Harriet) in September 1826, even consenting to meet him, though not his mother, the following May. From September 1827 she received £250 a year, increased eventually to £400, and Percy received similar amounts. The money was not a gift but a loan from the estate, repayable on Sir Timothy's death, and payment was often delayed. She managed, however, to realise one of her main ambitions, to pay for Percy's education, including his years at Harrow in the mid-1830s. (His aunt Claire was furious that he had been sent to Byron's old school; Shelley had been at Eton.)

Mary Shelley also earned money from her writing, but never enough to do without Sir Timothy's subsidies. Financially her novel *The Last Man* (1826) gained more than most of her undertakings. She sold the copyright to the publisher, Henry Colburn,

for £300. Shorter pieces – mainly book reviews, or romantic tales like 'The Invisible Girl' or 'The Heir of Mondolfo' – were generally less rewarding, imaginatively as well as financially, since they had to be tailored closely to the word-limits and readership of particular publications. Although she learned rapidly how to work within such limitations, she embarked on *The Last Man* hoping, she told Hunt in September 1823, 'that its clear water will wash off the mud of the magazines'.

The novel has some clear biographical resonances. 'The last man!' she noted in her journal on 14th May 1824. 'Yes I may well describe that solitary being's feelings, feeling myself as the last relic of a beloved race, my companions, extinct before me'. She was already working on the story, in which the narrator, Lionel Verney, eventually becomes the only human survivor of a plague which spreads through the world. The last survivor was a fairly common literary topic, partly in response to the ideas of Léopold Cuvier, who believed that current humanity was only one in a series of species which

The Last Man (1849), oil by John Martin. Martin produced a sketch of the same subject, now lost, in 1826, the year Mary Shelley's The Last Man *appeared. The theme of the last survivor was fairly popular in the literature and art of the first half of the nineteenth century.*

National Museums and Galleries on Merseyside, Walker Art Gallery

God successively created and destroyed. But the more personal significance of the idea was confirmed when, only a day after the diary entry on 'that solitary being', news reached England of Byron's death in Greece in April. Now disagreements at Genoa were forgiven or forgotten; her 'dear capricious fascinating' friend, whose 'faults being for the most part weaknesses induced one readily to pardon them', 'has become one of the people of the grave – that innumerable conclave to which the beings I best loved belong'. 'What do I here?' she asks. 'Why I am doomed to live on seeing all expire before me? ... At the age of twenty six I am in the condition of an aged person – all my old friends are gone'.

One aim of *The Last Man* was to memorialise the old friends. In the noble idealist Adrian, as Mary Shelley confirmed to one of her correspondents, she 'endeavoured, but how inadequately, to give some idea' of Shelley. Byron's physical attractiveness, sensuality and fascinating contradictions are one source for Lord Raymond, who wants a crown and dreams of out-doing Napoleon, yet cannot 'rule himself' in love. Parts of herself went into Verney, and her own role as interpreter for the others and as survivor is also made clear in the introduction to the novel, where another, unnamed narrator visits the cave of the ancient prophetess or sibyl by Lake Averno, as the Shelleys did, in 1818. Here the narrator and friend find piles of 'sibylline leaves', covered with writing in many languages, ancient and modern. They begin the work of ordering and deciphering these writings, which will become the story of the Last Man – a story which will take place at the end of the twenty-first century. The narrator carries on alone after the loss of 'the selected and matchless companion of her toils':

> *My labours have cheered long hours of solitude, and taken me out of a world, which has averted its once benignant face from me, to one glowing with imagination and power. ... I have been depressed, nay, agonised, at some parts of the recital, which I have faithfully transcribed from my materials. Yet such is human nature, that the excitement of mind was dear to me, and that the imagination, painter of tempest and earthquake or, worse, the stormy and ruin-fraught passions of man, softened my real sorrows and endless regrets, by clothing these fictitious ones in that ideality, which takes the mortal sting from pain.*

Both natural and man-made disasters abound in *The Last Man*. There is war as well as plague; human beings are as prone to 'ruin-fraught passions' as to disease. The rational Adrian, for instance, becomes insane for a time when the Greek princess Evadne cannot return his love. Evadne prefers Raymond; but his uncontrollable passion for her indirectly brings about his own and many other deaths. From the beginning their relationship has been bound up with power – not only sexual power, but political, since she is attracted by this forceful, individual man of affairs more than by the republican idealist Adrian.

The first of the three volumes of *The Last Man* is centrally concerned with political power. Britain becomes a republic in 2073 and towards the end of the century royalists, led by Adrian's mother, the former queen, are intriguing to regain power. Since Adrian himself is a convinced republican, they gravitate instead to the ambitious Raymond. Raymond and the republican leader, Ryland, debate in parliament whether those seeking to restore the monarchy should be charged with treason. (Mary Shelley prepared carefully for this passage by obtaining permission, through Byron's old friend John Cam Hobhouse, a member of parliament, to attend some debates at the House of Commons.) Ryland, in part a rather unsympathetic caricature of the radical journalist and campaigner William Cobbett, argues that monarchy tends 'to enslave the minds of men' while the republic has raised even the most humble citizen 'to something great and good'. He goes on to expose Raymond's designs on power. But in spite of his opponent's 'thunder of denunciations', Raymond defeats the motion, partly by argument – in practice the rich few rule the republic – but more by his 'graceful turns of expression', 'wit and easy raillery' and musical, enchanting voice.

Mary Shelley's sympathies were traditionally republican; her father had brought her up to be keenly aware of events and issues of the only period when, in the 1640s and 1650s, England had actually dispensed with monarchy. But she leaves the debate to speak for itself, and later in the novel, in any case, the progress of the plague puts all ideals, all power, into question. The British naively assume – in one of the author's glancing hits at the establishment – that the pestilence will not reach their island. When it does, Ryland, who has become Lord Protector following Raymond's death, dissolves into panic. He no longer wishes to 'protect or govern' the

Following pages:

The Forum viewed from the Farnese Gardens, by Camille Jean Baptiste Corot. Verney, near the end of The Last Man, *is 'alone in the Forum; alone in Rome; alone in the world'.*

Louvre/Bridgeman Art Library

87

hospital to which his country will speedily be reduced; where will his duties be when he is 'a plague-spotted corpse'? Adrian and Verney, by contrast, work on, doing what they can to fight the disease, sheltering refugees in Windsor Castle, and eventually deciding to lead the remaining inhabitants out of England in search of some healthier place. But in the end they can achieve nothing more than Ryland.

Some of the most poignant scenes in the novel occur while the main surviving characters wait for the plague to arrive. Verney comes back to Windsor from London, where the first symptoms have broken out. Young people are dancing to celebrate his son Alfred's birthday. 'At first the tripping measure lifted my spirit with it', but at once 'the revulsion of thought passed like keen steel to my heart': he realises that soon everyone he sees, including his own wife and children, will be dead. News that the plague is as near as London spreads and the dancers dissolve into whispering groups. Alfred 'stood immoveable, … his whole attention absorbed' by an Italian boy telling of scenes of plague he has witnessed. Verney's powerless horror at these scenes is, of course, influenced by the author's awareness of what it was to lose children and to remember times when, as she said in a journal entry of October 1822, 'their hands were warm with blood and life when clasped in mine'. And fear, principally for her remaining child, of some incurable, inexorably spreading disease, was understandable; in 1832 cholera, which had broken out in India fifteen years earlier, reached London and her younger brother, William Godwin Jr., was among those who died.

Towards the end Verney, as the reader has known he will, becomes the last man. His niece Clara, the last woman, drowns with Adrian when their boat is overwhelmed, like Shelley's, by a sudden storm. Shipwrecked near Ravenna, after a time Verney makes his way to Rome, 'the capital of the world, the crown of man's achievements'. Here he decides to write the story of his life. He dedicates it to 'the Illustrious Dead' and entertains the remote hope that somewhere people have survived and will one day read it. (According to the introduction, it is in fact people in the past who will decipher his account from the prophetic leaves. The questions raised by the book are, Mary Shelley suggests, of urgent contemporary relevance.) Finally he decides to sail down the Tiber; he will carry on the search for other human beings, knowing that it is probably futile but going on, 'for ever round another and another promontory, anchoring in another and another bay'.

'The genuine affections of the heart', 1826–40

Mary Shelley's remarks about her own position as the last survivor might suggest that she led a lonely and reclusive life in England. According to her friend Eliza Rennie, 'she was not a mirthful – scarcely could be called a cheerful – person; and, at times, was subject to ... profound fits of despondency, when she would shut herself up, and be quite inaccessible to all'. (Maria Jewsbury noted that she did laugh naturally in company, but that such hilarity contrasted strangely with 'the almost sadly profound nature of some of her remarks'.) Some areas of society, moreover, still frowned on her as irretrievably compromised by her premarital relationship with Shelley. Men were, on the whole, free to mix with such a woman, but it was regarded as unacceptable by, or for, some of the wives. Lord Dillon was her good friend, intrigued, he told her, that the author of 'such wild, imaginative novels' could seem 'so cool, quiet, feminine to the last degree', but many years later his widow saw fit to 'cut' or ignore her. Nevertheless she did move in a fairly wide social circle, increasingly including men and women who would probably not have wanted to know her in her more radical and bohemian youth. Lasting intimacies were, however, more difficult to maintain.

During the first few years back in England she invested much of her affection in Jane Williams. She was, according to a manuscript dedication for *The Last Man*, the 'dear solace of my life'. She may not have shown her friend the dedication; she was aware, although she often tried to hide it from herself, that Jane did not return her feelings with anything like the same intensity. But she needed a link with the idealised past, with Shelley and warm, longed-for Italy, and more simply needed someone in whom she felt she could confide.

There were times of mutual enjoyment. Both friends derived much pleasure, for instance, from the society of the musician and composer Vincent Novello and his family. Novello's daughter Mary, who was a teenager at the time, remembered, many years later, 'the two young and beautiful widows' and particularly Mrs Shelley's delight in listening to other guests' renderings of

Mozart arias and her 'caressing' way of asking 'Vincenzo' for her favourite music. She remembered her appearance in some detail:

> *her well-shaped, golden-haired head almost always a little bent and drooping; her marble white shoulders and arms statuesquely visible in the perfectly plain black velvet dress, which the customs of that time allowed to be cut low, and which her own taste adopted (for neither she nor her sister-in-sorrow ever wore the conventional 'widow's weeds' and 'widow's cap'); her thoughtful, earnest eyes; her short upper lip and intellectually curved mouth, with a certain closed, compressed and decisive expression while she listened, and a relaxation into fuller redness and mobility when speaking.*

'As I listen to music (especially instrumental),' she told Leigh Hunt, 'new ideas rise and develop themselves, with greater energy and truth than at any other time'.

But the monthly evenings of inspiration at the Novellos' came to an end for Mary Shelley in March 1828. Because some kind of rumour about her relationship with Novello was current, she wrote, with great reluctance, to break off their friendship. (Talk of a liaison with a married man would confirm Sir Timothy Shelley's impression of her and give him a good excuse to delay or cancel funds.) The friendship with Jane Williams was also, by then, in peril. Williams was probably not responsible for this particular rumour, but she still had a habit of spreading unkind gossip about her devoted friend.

Another reason for Mary Shelley's mounting feeling that she was being deserted was that Williams was, from 1827, living as the common law wife of Thomas Jefferson Hogg (once Shelley's preferred candidate for his own wife's attentions). In the summer of that year Isabel Robinson, a new friend, revealed some of the tales of Mary Shelley's coldness and inadequacy as a wife which Williams had gone on telling. 'My friend has proved false & treacherous!' records Mary Shelley in her journal on 13th July, but it was not until February 1828 that the poet Thomas Moore persuaded her that she must bring the matter to a head. An emotional scene followed, and after it a letter, more grieving than angry, to 'the sweet girl whose beauty, grace and gentleness were to me so long the sole charms of my life'.

Surprisingly, the friendship survived if in somewhat more moderate form. But the disloyalty of Jane Williams (or Jane Hogg as she now called herself) was one of the main factors in Mary Shelley's increasing belief, as she wrote to Maria Gisborne in 1835, that 'fidelity' is 'the first of human virtues'. She made it the main theme of her last novel, *Falkner* (1837).

Mary Shelley continued to write extensively amid the joys and perils of her friendships in the late 1820s: 'A Visit to Brighton', published by *The London Magazine* at the end of 1826, where she enjoys denigrating the resort's 'withered effigy of a park' and Kemp Town, an area so completely deserted that it might be 'the retreat of the "Last Man", reviews for the *Westminster Review*; several stories for the annual

Mary Shelley reflects on the different stages of Byron's literary career, in a letter of 1832 to the publisher John Murray.

The British Library, London, Add MS 38510, ff. 58v–9

its — the moon at palaces and the deserted ruined grandeurs of that city awakened the ruin that displayed itself in the 4th canto of C.H. in Mazeppa — in the Ode on Venice —

As his mind became more refined — he became more critical — but his school of criticism being of the narrow order; it confined his faculties in his tragedies & Lord Byron became sententious & dull — except where character still shone forth — or where his critical ideas did not tempt to Man — Sarcasm, before confined to his speech — now ~~stony~~ again

ing a sting from his & me... to the attacks made on him induced him to write the vision — & the ...tude in which he lived at Ravenna gave birth to deep thoughts — to fair — and Heaven & Earth —

At Pisa he again belonged more to the English world — It did him little good — because he wrote chiefly because he had for many years thought it a good subject. He was very anxious to go on with D. Juan — and verging on the time when people revert to past feelings, instead of dwelling on the present — he amused him

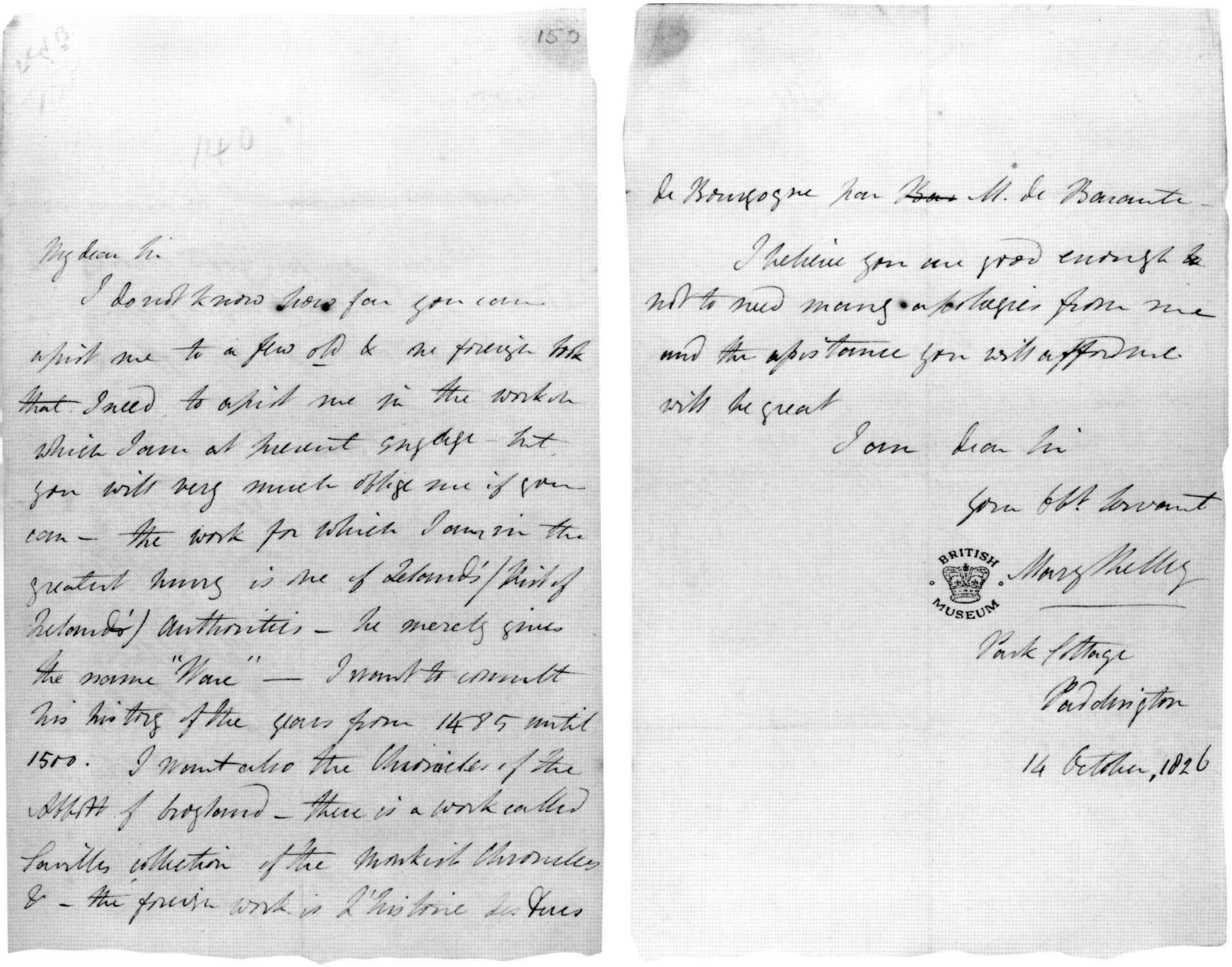

My dear Sir

I don't know how far you can assist me to a few old & no foreign books that I need to assist me in the works which I am at present engaged – but you will very much oblige me if you can – the work for which I am in the greatest hurry is one of Leland's (Philip of Ireland's) Authorities – he merely gives the name "Wace" – I want to consult his history of the years from 1485 until 1500. I want also the Chronicles of the Abbat of England – there is a work called Saville's collection of the English Chronicles & – the foreign work is L'histoire des Ducs de Bourgogne par M. de Barante –

I believe you are good enough to not to need many apologies from me and the assistance you will afford me will be great

I am dear Sir
Your obt. Servant
Mary Shelley

Park Cottage
Paddington
14 October, 1826

Keepsake; a second thoroughly researched historical novel, *The Fortunes of Perkin Warbeck* (1830). Her memories and editorial skills were also much in demand. She managed, unknown to Sir Timothy Shelley, to lend assistance to Cyrus Redding, editor of the *Poetical Works of Coleridge, Shelley and Keats*, published by Galignani of Paris in 1829. She helped Thomas Moore much more extensively with his *Letters and Journals of Lord Byron* (1830), gathering material and providing her own detailed recollections; she contributed much, here as in Moore's life of Byron (1832–35),

The Banqueting Room in Brighton Pavilion, by John Nash. In 'A Visit to Brighton' (1826), Mary Shelley says that George IV's exotic palace 'would have received the praise due to its elegance and picturesque effect' if only it had actually been in India or Persia rather than Brighton. She returned to the resort several times in the 1830s and 1840s.

The British Library, London, 557*b19

to the creation or recreation of, as she put it in a letter to the publisher, John Murray, 'our Lord Byron – the fascinating – faulty – childish – philosophical being' and the 'delightful and buoyant tone of his conversation and manners'.

Mary Shelley reached readers more directly with the revised *Frankenstein*. At six shillings, this one-volume edition was markedly cheaper than the 31 shillings usually charged for novels in the traditional three-volume or 'three-decker' format. It was published in October 1831 in the Bentley's Standard Novels series, which had also recently reissued works by Godwin. Within a year the new *Frankenstein* had sold 3,000 copies. The author badly needed the £60 Bentley paid her, but it seems fairly insubstantial in the light of the book's subsequent success.

While some revisions were simply stylistic improvements, a significant number altered the emphasis of the original work in the same direction as her editing of Shelley's poems: away from atheism and political radicalism, towards religion and

Portrait of Thomas Moore by Sir Thomas Lawrence. Moore, poet and biographer (with assistance from Mary Shelley) of his friend Byron, is best known for his Irish Melodies, *published between 1808 and 1834 and including 'The Last Rose of Summer'.*

John Murray

more conservative views. It is in the 1831 introduction that we first hear that Frankenstein's crime is to 'endeavour to mock the stupendous mechanism of the Creator of the world' and that he is a 'student of unhallowed arts'. In the novel itself Frankenstein now laments, perhaps under the influence of the author's memories of *Presumption*, that he has let loose on the world a 'living monument of presumption and rash ignorance'. To minimise possible suggestions of incest – one of the Shelleys' common themes, and a favourite accusation against their circle – Elizabeth is no longer Frankenstein's cousin. And the new version omits Elizabeth's passionate speech against the injustice of society, and of capital punishment in particular, to the condemned Justine.

William Godwin in old age, drawn by Daniel Maclise. Godwin, no longer seen as a dangerous figure, was at last freed from financial worry in his last years by his appointment to the sinecure post of Yeoman Usher of the Receipt of the Exchequer in 1833.

Victoria and Albert Museum, London

The new and more widely known *Frankenstein*, then, was less likely to be branded as extravagant, degenerate, 'presumptuous', than its predecessor. Mary Shelley was anxious not only to avoid provoking Sir Timothy more than necessary but also to avoid damaging her son's future prospects. For the same reason she delayed, and finally abandoned, the life of her father she agreed to produce soon after his death in 1836. Some of her acquaintance blamed her for such apparent timidity, and suspected that she was tepid in her support for the reformist causes dear to her parents and husband. Trelawny, who in one of his many incarnations was a member of a group of Philosophical Radicals in the 1830s, took it upon himself to be particularly disappointed with her. (His motives for attacking her mixed the personal and the political; he was frustrated, for instance, that she would not co-operate with him on a proposed biography of Shelley, and perhaps somewhat piqued that in order to make his own recollections publishable she had needed, while he was still abroad, to refine away elements of 'coarseness'.)

In October 1838 Trelawny's attacks prompted her to extended self-analysis in her journal. Where women's rights were concerned, she concluded, she could do most to fulfil her mother's ideals by personal acts of kindness to women who had fallen foul of the harsh morality of their contemporaries. One such woman was Isabel Robinson, an unmarried mother whom she had helped pass off in 1827 as the wife of 'Walter Sholto Douglas'. Douglas was in reality Diana Mary Dods, another friend for whom Mary Shelley felt more compassion than did most of her acquaintance. Dods was the neglected, illegitimate daughter of a nobleman. She suffered from what a mutual friend, Eliza Rennie, called 'some organic disease', and struck most people as distinctly masculine in manner and appearance. She was very probably lesbian.

Mary Shelley also did much to help Georgiana or 'Gee' Paul, who in 1831 was cast off by her husband for adultery, either actual or suspected. But, the 1838 journal entry continues, 'I do not make a boast – I do not say aloud – behold my generosity and greatness of mind – for in truth it is simple justice I perform – and so I am still reviled for being worldly'. Besides, 'the Rights of women' is a topic on which 'I am far from making up my mind'. It is perhaps fortunate that Trelawny was not present when, at a social gathering some weeks later, she told the American politician Charles Sumner that 'the greatest happiness for any woman [is] to be the wife or mother of a distinguished man'.

While remaining well aware of the case for 'the Rights of women', she continued to enjoy male company and actively considered remarrying. The main obstacle to this, she felt, was that the laws of society often impeded even friendship with the men in whom she was interested. One such was Bryan Waller Procter, a young poet 'whose voice, laden with sentiment, paused as Shelley's', and who 'bent his dark blue eyes upon me' for some months in 1823–24, but then simply stopped seeing her. Months later, she discovered from a newspaper that he had married another woman; no doubt it would have been compromising to have gone on seeing the attractive and not quite socially acceptable Mrs Shelley. The American playwright John Howard Payne, who lived in London, was more unequivocally in love with her, and proposed marriage in 1825. She did not share his feelings but managed, in spite of her refusal, to stay on good enough terms to go on taking enthusiastic advantage of the free theatre tickets he supplied.

In 1828, when she was stricken with smallpox while visiting Paris, she feared that she had lost the physical attractions on which she clearly prided herself; according to Rennie 'the pearly delicacy of her skin was gone for ever; and the fair luxuriant hair, thinned and dimmed by sickness, never recovered its former

The American playwright John Howard Payne in later life. He knew Mary Shelley from 1823 until 1832, when he returned to the United States after an absence of nearly twenty years.

The British Library, London, 10880g24

Mary Shelley

Edmund Kean (1787–1833), the foremost tragic actor of his day, as Shakespeare's Richard III. 'To see him act', according to Coleridge, was 'like reading Shakespeare by flashes of lightning'. Mary Shelley saw him in most of his major roles.

Victoria and Albert Museum, London

abundance and gloss'. But soon afterwards, pearl-skinned or not, she was enjoying a flirtation with the French writer Prosper Mérimée, who later wrote *Carmen*, the tale reworked for Bizet's opera. Distinctly more cautious than Carmen, Mary Shelley politely declined taking their contact beyond flirtation. Instead, she promoted Mérimée's work in England in two long pieces for the *Westminster Review*.

Possibly in France, where she was delighted that men of letters gave her a warm reception of the sort not granted by their more propriety-conscious English equivalents, she talked a little more than usual about her work. At home, if Rennie is to be believed, 'she was morbidly averse to the least allusion to herself' as a writer.

Whether Mary Shelley discussed her work with Major Aubrey Beauclerk is unknown. It was also unknown, until the 1980s, that she had high hopes of marrying him. Beauclerk, who was Gee Paul's brother, was a wealthy and well-connected liberal member of parliament. In the spring of 1833 Mary Shelley seems keenly to have been expecting a proposal of marriage, only to hear, probably in August, that he was instead to marry the younger and richer Ida Goring. She speaks cryptically in her journal of 'frightful calamity'. For some months she was distraught, but 'the friendship and gratitude of Gee have been very soothing'. On the Beauclerks' wedding-day, 13th February 1834, she wrote simply 'Farewell', and a year later observed the 'strange and sad! – and bitter' anniversary. When Ida Beauclerk died in 1838 Mary Shelley nourished at least a faint hope that now Beauclerk would marry her, but this time, in 1841, he chose her friend Rosa Robinson, sister of Isabel. This may have been one reason why the much longer friendship with a third Robinson sister, Julia, foundered in 1842. More immediately, however, the break came because Julia Robinson claimed that her family 'had sacrificed a brilliant society' for Mary Shelley's sake.

Some 'brilliant society' features in the novel Mary Shelley wrote between 1831 and 1834, *Lodore*, where most of the characters are aristocrats. But here, as not in the fashionable 'silver-fork' or high society novels produced by some of her contemporaries, rank and wealth bring with them serious difficulties; 'cloyed by the too easy attainment of the necessaries, and even of the pleasures, of life, they fly to the tortures of passion'. Lord Lodore, after foreign travel, an affair with a Polish countess and much boredom, marries Cornelia, an impoverished sixteen-year-old of good family whose main motive for accepting him is the desire for the status, riches and glamorous social life which come with him. She is encouraged in this attitude by her manipulative mother. Cornelia, much involved in fashionable society, pays little attention to their young daughter, Ethel. This is why, although his decision is not presented as a wise one, Lodore takes Ethel with him to live in Illinois when an affair of honour forces him to leave England. Cornelia, under her mother's influence, had refused to go with him. In America Lodore cares for, and carefully educates, his daughter. But in common with many girls she does not learn sufficiently 'to rely on and act for herself'. They live a mostly secluded life, and only when Ethel is in danger of falling in love with an unsuitable man does he realise that 'the village in the Illinois was not the scene fitted for' the social development of 'one so pure, so guileless, and so inexperienced'. Accordingly, in search of more 'educated and refined' society, they go to New York with a view to returning to Europe, but a chance meeting with someone who believes that Lodore left England simply out of cowardice leads to a duel in which Lodore is killed. Much though Ethel mourns him, he has died for nothing and has left her little prepared for her future life.

Ethel has already, however, met Fanny Derham, a young woman whose late father provided her with a more useful education, and who is often, as a result, able to come to her support. Fanny has learned the lessons of Wollstonecraft and Godwin: to be 'complete in herself', 'independent and self-sufficing', and 'to penetrate, to anatomize, to purify my motives; but once assured of my own integrity, to be afraid of nothing'. With Edward Villiers, a young Englishman who acted as Lodore's second in the fatal duel, and who later marries Ethel, they travel back to England. Villiers, although he is in many ways a sympathetic, partly Shelley-derived figure, is – also like Shelley sometimes – 'imprudent from his belief in the goodness of his fellow-creatures'. His generosity to his spendthrift, irresponsible father helps to make him and Ethel poor. (It is during their enforced separations, similar to those the Shelleys had experienced when they too were pursued by the bailiffs, that Ethel, although she shows some courage herself, most needs Fanny's wisdom and support.) He also puts too much value on the way poverty makes others perceive him, since 'We rate each individual ... not by himself, but by his house, his park, his income'. Ethel is aware that this is the wrong way to judge. Nevertheless their love holds,

The opening page of
volume 2, chapter 1, of
Mary Shelley's Lodore
(1835).

The British Library,
London, N.1134

> # LODORE.
>
> ---
>
> ## CHAPTER I.
>
> Excellent creature! whose perfections make
> Even sorrow lovely!
>
> BEAUMONT AND FLETCHER.
>
> MR. Villiers now became the constant visitor of
> Mrs. Elizabeth and her niece; and all discontent,
> all sadness, all listlessness, vanished in his pre-
> sence. There was in his mind a constant spring of
> vivacity, which did not display itself in mere
> gaiety, but in being perfectly alive at every
> moment, and continually ready to lend himself
> to the comfort and solace of his companions.
>
> VOL. II.   B

their luck changes, and by the end he has learned 'to prize worldly prosperity at its face value'.

Meanwhile Cornelia, Lady Lodore, has gone through a more painful learning process. The death of her mother, glimpses of the daughter who has so long lived apart from her, and compassion for her difficulties, make her increasingly dissatisfied

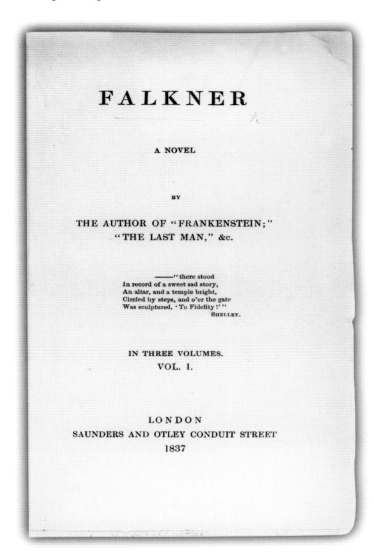

FALKNER

A NOVEL

BY

THE AUTHOR OF "FRANKENSTEIN;"
"THE LAST MAN," &c.

———" there stood
In record of a sweet sad story,
An altar, and a temple bright,
Circled by steps, and o'er the gate
Was sculptured, 'To Fidelity !'"
SHELLEY.

IN THREE VOLUMES.
VOL. I.

LONDON
SAUNDERS AND OTLEY CONDUIT STREET
1837

Title-page of Mary Shelley's last novel Falkner *(1837). The main theme of the novel is fidelity. This, she told her friend Marcia Gisborne, is the most important of human virtues.*

The British Library, London, N.1397

with her own elegant but empty life. With much anguish, she decides to give up her property and wealth to her daughter. After various further vicissitudes mother and daughter are brought happily together. Lady Lodore marries a deserving former suitor who regards her new-found intense maternal love as 'her crowning virtue'. She has found, as Mary Shelley put it to Charles Ollier in January 1833, 'all to be vanity, except the genuine affections of the heart'.

Reviewers on the whole liked *Lodore*. *The Courier*, for instance, was relieved to encounter this 'more natural' successor to Mary Shelley's earlier 'wild fictions', and for *The Sunday Times* it was 'an affecting tale of domestic affections and every-day life'. But neither *Lodore* (1835) nor its successor *Falkner* (1837) sold particularly well, and she wrote no more novels. Already in 1834 she had written of the therapeutic benefits of working on material less emotionally engaging than fiction. She had been commissioned by Rev. Dionysius Lardner, an acquaintance of her father, to write the greater part of *Lives of the Most Eminent Literary and Scientific Men of Italy, Spain and Portugal* (1835–37) and the companion volume on equivalent French figures (1838–39). Such work helped her to cope with her periodical 'accesses almost intolerable of low spirits or ennui', which were brought on partly by the loss of Aubrey Beauclerk. In December 1834 she went so far as to claim that 'my life and reason have been saved by these "Lives".'

In a matter of months she produced, for the first of the five volumes, substantial accounts of Petrarch, Boccaccio, and Machiavelli, and shorter essays on a number of other early Italian writers. In the winter of 1834–35 continued labour on later Italians

LIVES of the most EMINENT LITERARY AND SCIENTIFIC MEN OF FRANCE. VOL. 1.

London:
PRINTED FOR LONGMAN, ORME, BROWN, GREEN, & LONGMANS, PATERNOSTER ROW,
AND JOHN TAYLOR, UPPER GOWER STREET.
1838.

*Title-page to Mary
Shelley's anonymously
published* Lives of the
Most Eminent
Literary and Scientific
Men of France, *volume 1 (1838). She
told the publisher
Edward Moxon that she
thought she did such
'quieter work ... much
better than romancing'.*

*The British Library, London,
12203.tt.1(33)*

for the second volume contributed to the exhaustion and depression she records in March, but the deeper cause of this was a sense that there was no-one with whom she could relax from her work, or obtain sympathy. (The fifteen-year-old Percy cared for her, but exhibited little interest in her writing.) She recovered to write many more of the Lives. Sadly, they have never been republished. Their achievement is to digest a considerable range of foreign-language material into highly readable English accounts. Her lifetime of reading, together with more immediate research and, for the Italian sections, local knowledge, made her a suitable choice for the undertaking. And as in *Lodore* she took the occasional opportunity to raise issues without appearing to depart from her more conventional brief. She introduces Vittoria Colonna, for instance, the only woman allowed to slip in among the 'Eminent Men' of the first three volumes, by way of a rapid, enthusiastic tour of other, often neglected, Italian female writers and scholars.

Mary Shelley's most influential late work, however, was her editions of Shelley's *Poetical Works* and *Essays, Letters from Abroad, Translations and Fragments*, both published in 1839. The continuing appearance of unauthorised editions finally persuaded Sir Timothy to withdraw his opposition to her involvement in 1838. Since his veto on biography still stood, she decided to include in *Poetical Works* 'a few notes appertaining to the history of the poems'. In these notes, or short essays, she was able to produce, while observing the letter of her father-in-law's decree, the elements of a life. This format also made it easier to avoid awkward areas like Shelley's first marriage, the date of his second, and the couple's near-estrangement at the end of his life.

The notes revisit their years together, sometimes painfully – at points she felt 'torn to pieces by Memory' – sometimes in more celebratory vein. In the process she is able to shape Shelley's life, giving it an order and pattern less evident at the time or in the anguished meditations of her journal afterwards. She also shaped the reception of his poetry. Her introduction to *Poetical Works*, together with briefer comments in the notes, went far to establish the Victorian image of Shelley as a spiritual, suffering, essentially virtuous being and as a poet of nature as much as of politics. (She did not ignore his evident political views but endeavoured to place them in their particular historical and personal context.) In places she adopts an almost religious tone:

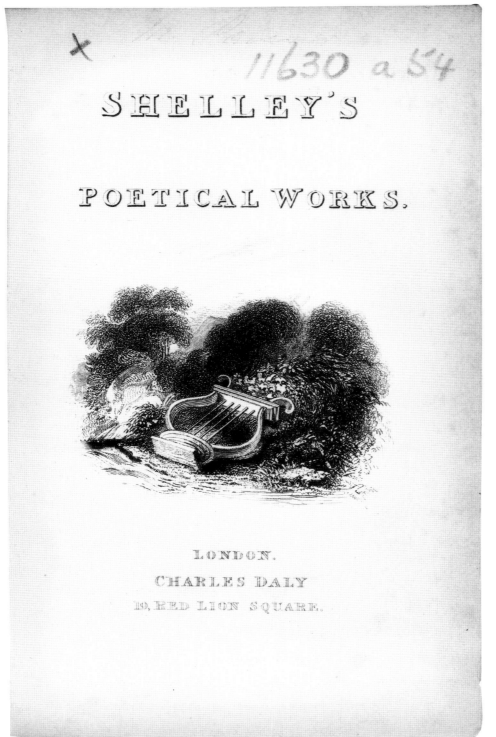

SHELLEY'S

POETICAL WORKS.

LONDON.

CHARLES DALY

19, RED LION SQUARE.

The title-page of volume 1 of Percy Bysshe Shelley's, Poetical Works *(1839), edited by Mary Shelley. This edition was chiefly responsible for establishing Shelley's reputation as a poet.*

The British Library, London, 11630.a.54

He died, and the world showed no outward sign. But his influence over mankind, though slow in growth, is fast augmenting ... He died, and his place, among those who knew him intimately, has never been filled up. He walked beside them like a spirit of good to comfort and benefit – to enlighten the darkness of life with irradiations of genius, to cheer it with his sympathy and love. ... It is our best consolation to know that such a pure-minded and exalted being was once among us, and now exists where we hope one day to join him.

As Shelley's editor she fulfilled what she saw as her duty to him, possibly as an atonement for the state of her relations with him at his death, possibly too as a way of making her loss of hope for a second marriage more palatable as she revisited and re-ordered her first.

Rambles and 'Unreserved directness', 1840–51

Poetical Works yielded Mary Shelley £500. Money problems remained, however, some occasioned by her frequent periods of ill-health – persistent influenza and then, from 1839, the early symptoms of a slowly developing brain tumour. Another financial pressure was the need to educate and maintain Percy at Harrow and then, between 1837 and 1840, at Trinity College, Cambridge. Sir Timothy, however, liked his grandson on the few occasions when they met, and began to contribute more generously.

At the same time Percy contributed, increasingly, to his mother's general well-being. He showed no signs of following in the footsteps of his illustrious forebears, except in so far as he shared his father's passion for boating. The diarist Henry Crabb Robinson dismissed him, when he was nineteen, as 'a loutish-looking boy, quite unworthy of his intellectual ancestors in appearance'. But his affection and general steadiness were not in doubt. In 1834 Mary Shelley was able to describe him to Maria Gisborne as 'trustworthy and thoughtful beyond his years'; by 1844, she told Claire Clairmont, he was 'the sheet anchor of my life'.

In the summer of 1840 financial difficulties had receded sufficiently for mother and son to visit the Continent with several of Percy's friends. They went, by way of Paris and Germany, to Lake Como. Here Percy's sailing caused her some anxiety, but she deeply enjoyed her first encounter with Italy for seventeen years, and dreaded the return to the isolation and poverty of 'chill dark England' from her 'summer-night's-dream of ambrosial, gentle airs, and shadowing groves – and lake and craggy height'. It was in October, when the young men had gone ahead and she was travelling home more slowly with her maid, that she had a more unsettling glimpse of the past. From a steamer on Lake Léman she saw Villa Diodati and Maison Chapuis. She wrote about the experience in *Rambles in Germany and Italy* (1844):

> *There were the terraces, the vineyards, the upward path threading them, the little port where our boat lay moored; I could mark and recognise a thousand slight peculiarities ... Was I the same person who had lived there, the companion of the dead? For all were gone ... and now I looked on the inanimate objects that had surrounded me, which survived, the same in aspect as then, to feel that all my life since was but an unreal phantasmagoria.*

Mary and Percy Shelley returned to Germany and Italy for a longer visit between June 1842 and August 1843. One reason for this was the hope that German spas and Italian warmth might cure or alleviate her increasing illness. She complained frequently of headaches. She also sometimes found it difficult to cope

Opposite page:

A week before going abroad with her son Percy in June 1840, Mary Shelley writes from Brighton to Marianne Hunt about Leigh Hunt's play A Legend of Florence, *Sir Timothy Shelley's longevity, and Percy as 'the comfort and charm of my life'.*

The British Library, London, Add MS 38523, ff. 220

with Percy's two companions, Alexander Knox and Henry Pearson, themselves ill and irritable and neither of them very close to the shy or self-contained Percy. Pearson was much the more troublesome of the two, and there was general relief when he left the party in November 1842.

In addition to coping with pain and young men and touring art galleries, she took notes about the people and politics of the countries she visited. 'Knowledge, to enlighten and free the mind from clinging, deadening prejudices – a wider circle of sympathy with our fellow creatures – these are the uses of travel,' she says in *Rambles*, the idea for which took clearer shape as a result of her introduction, in 1843, to a group of Italian political exiles in Paris. Fired by sympathy with their suffering in the cause of independence, and a determination to raise money to help them (particularly Ferdinando Gatteschi), she wrote quickly, although often in pain. One of her aims is to attack not just the Austrian and other rulers of Italy but the traditional English contempt for 'the effeminacy of the Italians'. They are 'made to be a free, active, inquiring people', she believes, but while their rulers

The German spa town Baden-Baden. Mary Shelley visited briefly in 1840 and spent the summer of 1847 here in an unsuccessful attempt to recover her health.

The British Library, London, 10108.de.18

deprive them of education and the power of self-determination how can they realise this potential?

Some reviewers liked such departures from the usual chronicling the sights to 'the higher subject of national character'. Most responses were fairly favourable, but the more conservative *Observer* felt that for women 'politics is a matter of the heart ... and consequently her arguments take the tone of passion, and her convictions the tone of personal feeling. It is an idle and unprofitable theme for a woman'. *Rambles* was Mary Shelley's last work of any substance. Possibly realising that this might be the case, she ends it not with some proclamation to annoy the man from the *Observer*, but with Shelley's old symbol for her, the moon: above Sorrento 'the moon hangs luminous, a pendant sphere of silver fire'.

While she was working on the travel book, on 24th April 1844, Sir Timothy Shelley died at the age of ninety and Percy succeeded to the baronetcy and estate.

A contemporary map of the Bay of Naples. Mary Shelley, Percy Florence Shelley and Alexander Knox stayed in Sorrento between May and July 1843.

The British Library, London, 568.f.16

His mother was pleased at his new status, but the inheritance did not supply quite the degree of affluence she had sometimes allowed herself to expect. £500 a year was required for the widowed Elizabeth, Lady Shelley. The £13,000 loaned over the last twenty years to Mary and Percy Shelley must be repaid to the estate. Then there were Shelley's debts and legacies to be met, including substantial sums for Claire Clairmont, Ianthe Esdaile (his daughter by Harriet) and Leigh Hunt.

An advantage of Sir Percy Shelley's new position and prospects, however, was the ease with which he could borrow money. He was also able to sell a Shelley family property, Castle Goring, for £11,250. The legacies were paid out in 1844–45. What finally kept the Shelleys solvent, however, was Percy's marriage, in 1848, to Jane St John, a young widow with a fortune of £15,000. She struck her mother-in-law as 'the sweetest creature I ever knew, so affectionate, so soft – she looks what she is, all goodness and truth'. But she also had qualities of determination lacking in Percy, and took over responsibility for presenting the image of both his parents to the public: policing or seeing off biographers and editing out inconvenient facts. Mary Shelley had found a woman she could unreservedly trust.

She could, as her relationship with Jane Williams had shown, be too trusting. In September 1845 Ferdinando Gatteschi tried to take advantage of this characteristic – the 'unreserved directness towards those she regarded with affection' later described by the Hunts' eldest son, Thornton. Gatteschi attempted to blackmail her, threatening to make her letters to him public. No doubt the letters were full of enthusiasm for Italian nationalism and affection for him as an unjustly persecuted but romantic exile from the beloved country. Such sentiments could easily be misconstrued. Mary Shelley's precarious reputation was under threat; it had been slowly recovering, for some years, from her earlier image as the daughter of dangerous parents and licentious mistress of the infidel Shelley. Her shock and anxiety probably exacerbated her suffering from 'what my physician calls functional derangement in the nerves or brain'.

The anxiety lasted about a month. Her travelling companion of two years earlier, Alexander Knox, was in Paris and charged himself with the responsibility of extricating her from Gatteschi's clutches. She sent Knox the menacing letters, unopened, as they arrived. In Paris he discussed how to proceed with Claire

Clairmont, who had been living in Paris for several years. More importantly, he consulted the city authorities. On 11th October, with remarkable efficiency, the prefect of police, Gabriel Delessert, seized all the Italian's papers – for political reasons, he let it be known – and allowed Knox to remove the letters.

Another agitating event of her last years had its roots much further in her past. Relations with Claire Clairmont had continued to fluctuate. They saw each other from time to time in either Paris or London, and frequently exchanged letters. Sometimes the old tensions surfaced. Their contrasting attitudes to Byron's memory was one bone of contention: on 15 March 1836, in her usual vigorous style, Clairmont told her stepsister that

> *I stick to Frankenstein, merely because that vile spirit does not haunt its pages as it does in all your other novels, now as Castruccio, now as Raymond, now as Lodore. Good God, to think that a person of your genius, whose moral tact ought to be proportionately exalted, should think it a task befitting its powers to gild and embellish and pass off as beautiful what was the merest compound of vanity, folly, and every miserable weakness that ever met together in one human being.*

Such anger is understandable, given the loss of Allegra. There were, however, less accountable outbursts and jealousies. In the early summer of 1849 Clara Clairmont, the twenty-three-year-old daughter of Claire's brother Charles, who had settled in Vienna, came to stay with the Shelleys at Field Place, the family home in Sussex. Knox was already staying there, and he and Clara fell in love. Very soon, on 16th June, they were married in London. The girl's aunt at first seemed to accept the match, but then started issuing furious letters to the family. The marriage had gone ahead without Clara's parents' permission, and, worse, without her aunt being informed. Because she had somehow convinced herself that Knox was Mary Shelley's lover, she accused her of masterminding the marriage and at last, at the age of fifty-one, broke off all communication with her. Clairmont remained offended with the younger Shelleys for years afterwards. A story told later by Jane Shelley suggests the depth of antagonism between the stepsisters even before this final break. During

*Field Place, Sussex.
Sir Percy Florence Shelley
inherited the house and
estate, where his father
had grown up, in 1844.
This engraving appeared
in Thomas Jefferson
Hogg's* The Life of
Percy Bysshe Shelley
(1858).

*The British Library, London,
2408.aa.6*

a visit by Clairmont to Field Place, they were about to be left together when, with surprising passion, Mary Shelley pleaded with her daughter-in-law, 'Don't go, dear! don't leave me alone with her! She has been the bane of my life ever since I was three years old!'

Throughout the 1840s Mary Shelley's health had gradually declined. She suffered a major attack of some sort in November 1848. At her doctor's recommendation she spent the winter of 1849-50 in Nice, with Sir Percy and Lady Shelley – also seeking improved health at the time. She sometimes felt well enough to ride into the hills on a donkey, but was becoming evidently more frail. They moved on to Lake Como in the spring, but did not stay long. By now 'inability to walk and nervous spasms are my chief ills', she wrote to her old friend Isabella Baxter Booth. Writing was painful and confined to letters.

In the autumn of 1850 the Shelleys left Field Place, which they found damp and dull, for their house at 24 Chester Square, London. Here, after a series of seizures, Mary Shelley went into a coma on 23rd January 1851. She died on 1st February without regaining consciousness, aged fifty-three. Her death certificate gave the cause of death as 'Disease of the Brain Supposed Tumour in left hemisphere, of long standing'; modern

Sir Percy Florence Shelley aged sixty, in 1879.

Hulton Archive

*Henry Weekes'
monument to the
Shelleys at Christchurch
Priory, Dorset, near the
home of her son and
daughter-in-law at
Boscombe.*

Hulton Archive

studies suggest that the correct diagnosis is probably meningioma, where a tumour originates in the covering of the brain and grows slowly into the brain itself. She was buried a week later at St Peter's Church, Bournemouth, near the new Shelley home at Boscombe. She had wanted to be buried with her parents, and so the remains of Mary Wollstonecraft and William Godwin were transferred there from the disused St Pancras churchyard. At an unknown date between then and 1889 another important link was reasserted when Sir Percy Shelley also placed in the tomb the ashes of his father's heart.

Most of Mary Shelley's work was neglected between her death and the new scholarly interest which began in the 1980s. But *Frankenstein*, the 'hideous progeny' which she bade 'go forth and prosper' in her introduction, lived on after 1851. The most famous offspring were the film versions directed by James Whale, *Frankenstein*

(1931), and its sequel *The Bride of Frankenstein* (1935). Boris Karloff was the definitive bolt-necked monster. Elaborate machinery was now available to animate him, and Frankenstein became the mad scientist of twentieth-century tradition, with his repeated cries of 'It's alive!' In spite of, or often because of, these and subsequent films, people have gone on reading the more complex original.

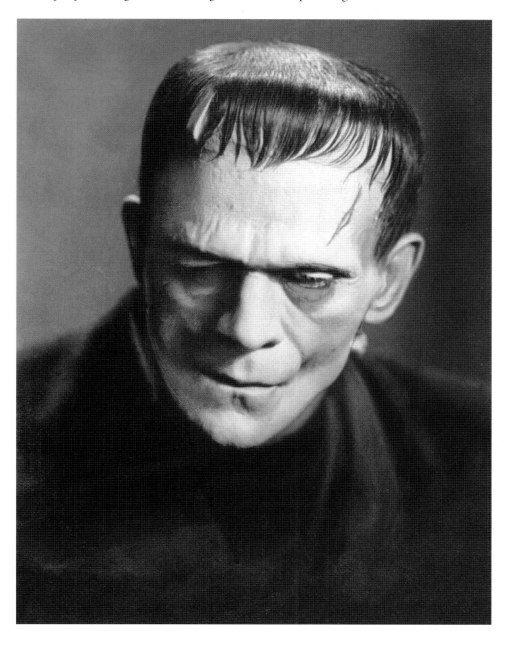

Boris Karloff as the monster in Frankenstein *(1931), directed by James Whale.*

Daily Herald Archive/ NMPFT/Science and Society Picture Library

*Posthumous portrait
of Mary Shelley: a
miniature by
Reginald Easton.*

Bodleian Library, Oxford

Mary Shelley 1797–1851
Chronology

1797	30th August: birth of Mary Wollstonecraft Godwin at 29 The Polygon, Somers Town
	10th September: death of her mother, Mary Wollstonecraft (1759–97)
1801	Mary Godwin's father, William (1756–1836), marries Mary Jane Clairmont (1768–1841)
1811	Mary Godwin spends several weeks in Ramsgate
1812	She stays with the Baxters at Broughty Ferry, near Dundee
1812	11th November: first meeting with Percy Bysshe Shelley (1792–1822)
1813–14	Second visit to the Baxters
1814	5th May: Mary Godwin meets Shelley again
	July: the couple leave for France, taking with them Mary Godwin's stepsister, Claire Clairmont (1798–1879)
	They go on to Switzerland and Germany
1814–16	Mary Godwin and Shelley live at various addresses in London and then at Bishopsgate, near Windsor
1815	Battle of Waterloo
1816	Birth of William Shelley
	The family goes to Switzerland, where they see much of George Gordon, Lord Byron (1788–1824) and Mary Godwin begins *Frankenstein*
1816–18	They live in Bath, London and Marlow
1816	Suicide of Mary Godwin's half-sister, Fanny, and Shelley's first wife, Harriet
	30th December: marriage of Mary Godwin and Shelley
1817	Birth of Allegra Byron and Clara Shelley. *History of a Six Weeks' Tour*
1818	*Frankenstein*. The Shelleys and Claire Clairmont settle in Italy
	Death of Clara Shelley

1819	Death of William Shelley. 'Peterloo' massacre
	Birth of Percy Florence Shelley
1819–20	Mary Shelley writes *The Fields of Fancy*, revised as *Matilda*
1820	She writes *Proserpine*, *Midas* and 'Maurice, or The Fisher's Cot'
1821	The Shelleys become friends with Edward and Jane Williams in Pisa
1822	They meet Edward John Trelawny
	Death of Shelley and Edward Williams
1823	*Valperga*. Mary Shelley returns to England
	Presumption, based on *Frankenstein*, performed
1824	Death of Byron. Shelley's *Posthumous Poems*
1826	*The Last Man*
1828	Visit to Paris
1830	*Perkin Warbeck*. Thomas Moore's *Letters and Journals of Lord Byron*
1831	Revised *Frankenstein*
1832–35	Moore's life of Byron
1833	Mary Shelley hopes to marry Aubrey Beauclerk
1835–37	Italian, Spanish and Portuguese *Lives*
1835	*Lodore*
1836	Death of William Godwin
1837	Victoria becomes Queen. *Falkner*
1838–39	French *Lives*
1839	Editions of Shelley's *Poetical Works* and prose
	Mary Shelley's health begins to decline
1840 and	
1842-43	Mary and Percy Florence Shelley travel in Germany and Italy
1844	Death of Sir Timothy Shelley. Percy Florence succeeds as baronet
	Rambles in Italy and Germany
1845	Blackmail attempt by Ferdinando Gatteschi
1849	Final quarrel with Claire Clairmont
1851	1st February: death of Mary Shelley at 24 Chester Square, London
1879	Death of Claire Clairmont
1889	Death of Sir Percy Florence Shelley

Further Reading

WORKS BY MARY SHELLEY

The Journals of Mary Shelley 1814–1844, ed. Paula R. Feldman and
Diana Scott-Kilvert, 2 vols (Clarendon Press, Oxford, 1987)

The Letters of Mary Wollstonecraft Shelley, ed. Betty T. Bennett, 3 vols
(Johns Hopkins University Press, Baltimore and London, 1980–88)

Mary Shelley, Novels and Selected Works, ed. Nora Crook, 8 vols
(Pickering, London, 1996)

Frankenstein or the Modern Prometheus: the 1818 Text, ed. Marilyn Butler
(Oxford University Press, Oxford, 1993)

The 'Frankenstein Notebooks': a Facsimile Edition of Mary Shelley's Manuscript Novel,
1816–17, ed. Charles E. Robinson, 2 vols
(Garland, New York and London, 1996)

Maurice; or The Fisher's Cot, ed. Claire Tomalin (Viking, London, 1998)

Mary Shelley: Collected Tales and Stories, ed. Charles E. Robinson
(Johns Hopkins University Press, Baltimore and London, 1976)

BIOGRAPHY

*Lives of the Great Romantics 3: Godwin, Wollstonecraft and Mary Shelley by their
contemporaries*, ed. Pamela Clemit, Harriet Devine Jump and Betty T. Bennett, 3 vols
(Pickering and Chatto, London, 1999)

Martin Garrett, *A Mary Shelley Chronology*
(Palgrave, Basingstoke, and St Martin's Press, New York, 2002)

Richard Holmes, *Shelley: the Pursuit* (Weidenfeld and Nicolson, London, 1974)

William St Clair, *The Godwins and the Shelleys: the Biography of a Family*
(Faber and Faber, London, 1989)

Miranda Seymour, *Mary Shelley* (John Murray, London, 2000)

Emily W. Sunstein, *Mary Shelley: Romance and Reality*
(Johns Hopkins University Press, Baltimore, 1989)

Also useful on Mary Shelley's life are *The Journals of Claire Clairmont*,
ed. Marion Kingston Stocking (Harvard University Press, Cambridge, Mass., 1968)
and *The Clairmont Correspondence: Letters of Claire Clairmont, Charles Clairmont,
and Fanny Imlay Godwin*,
ed. Marion Kingston Stocking, 2 vols (Johns Hopkins University Press,
Baltimore and London, 1995)

OTHER IMPORTANT STUDIES

Chris Baldick, *In Frankenstein's Shadow: Myth, Monstrosity and Nineteenth-Century Writing* (Clarendon Press, Oxford, 1987)

Betty T. Bennett, *Mary Wollstonecraft Shelley: an Introduction* (Johns Hopkins University Press, Baltimore and London, 1998)

Jane Blumberg, *Mary Shelley's Early Novels: 'This Child of Imagination and Misery'* (Macmillan, London, 1993)

The Other Mary Shelley: Beyond Frankenstein, ed. Audrey A. Fisch, Anne K. Mellor and Esther H. Schor (Oxford University Press, Oxford and New York, 1993)

Steven Earl Forry, *Hideous Progenies: Dramatizations of 'Frankenstein' from Mary Shelley to the Present* (Pennsylvania University Press, Philadelphia, 1990)

Christopher Frayling, *Nightmare: the Birth of Horror* (BBC Books, London, 1996)

John Williams, *Mary Shelley: a Literary Life* (Macmillan, Basingstoke and London, and St Martin's Press, New York, 2000)

≈ *Index*

Acknowledgements

I should like to thank Helen, Philip and Edmund for their encouragement, and Lara Speicher and Kathleen Houghton of the British Library Publishing Office for their useful advice, attention to detail, and hard work on the text and pictures of this book.

The British Library is grateful to Bodleian Library, Oxford, the Board of Trustees of the National Museums and Galleries on Merseyside (Walker Art Gallery, Liverpool), the British Museum, Guildhall Library, Corporation of London, John Murray (Publishers) Ltd, the Trustees of the National Portrait Gallery, Newstead Abbey, New York Public Library, Victoria and Albert Museum, the Louvre/Bridgeman Art Library, Hulton Archive and other named copyright holders for permission to reproduce illustrations

Front cover illustrations:	*Scene at Pompeii*, 1815 (The British Library, London 568.f.16) *Mary Shelley* by Richard Rothwell (National Portrait Gallery, London) Title-page to the 1818 edition of *Frankenstein* (The British Library, London, N751.9076624)
Back cover illustrations:	*Mary Shelley* by Richard Rothwell (National Portrait Gallery, London) *Villa Diodati* (John Murray)
Half-title page:	*Mary Shelley* by Richard Rothwell (National Portrait Gallery, London)
Frontispiece:	Title-page to the 1831 edition of *Frankenstein* (The British Library, London, 1153.a.9(1))
Contents page:	*Scene at Pompeii*, 1815 (The British Library, London, 568.f.16)

Text © 2002 Martin Garrett

Illustrations © 2002 The British Library Board and other named copyright holders

Published in the United States of America by
Oxford University Press, Inc.
198 Madison Avenue
New York, NY 10016
www.oup.com
Oxford is a registered trademark of Oxford University Press, Inc.
ISBN 0-19-521789-6

First published 2002 by The British Library, 96 Euston Road, London NW1 2DB

Designed and typeset by Crayon Design, Stoke Row, Henley-on-Thames
Maps by John Mitchell
Colour and black and white origination by Crayon Design and South Sea International Press
Printed in Hong Kong by South Sea International Press